UNSETTLED
DISRUPTION

Juana-Catalina Rodriguez is a serial intrapreneur and entrepreneur. She had developed multiple innovation projects in several industries, including fast-moving consumer goods, retail, financial services, mobile retail, cloud storage, digital identities, digital transformation, and social innovation across Asia-Pacific, Europe, Latin America, and North America. She is a startup advisor, author, and founder of JnC Nova. This company helps startups, intrapreneurs, and other innovators accelerate their development and grow their businesses by streamlining their innovation processes. Juana-Catalina is an executive coach for the Stanford GSB Seed-Stanford Institute for Innovation in Developing Economies and Stanford GSB LEAD for global executives and entrepreneurs.

PRAISE FOR *UNSETTLED DISRUPTION*

"As a leader with a knack for embracing and embellishing change, I find that *Unsettled Disruption* by Juana-Catalina Rodriguez has given me another grounded and logical approach to 'purpose-driven disruptive' thinking. I loved it. For leaders who support collaboration and like to kick the tires of new ideas, read this book . . . not once, but twice. And take lots of notes."

—**Dr. Troy Hall,** Global Speaker, Radio Host, Talent-Retention Strategist, Best-Selling Author of *Cohesion Culture: Proven Principles to Retain Your Top Talent*

"With her practical *Unsettled Disruption* framework, Juana-Catalina empowers you to become a real disruptor of any sector."

—**Gijs van Wulfen**, Innovation Expert, Best-Selling Author of *The Innovation Maze* and *The Innovation Expedition*

"Kudos to Juana-Catalina for talking about disruption in a transparent and honest way. Her approach to innovation thinking using different frameworks to truly break away from analysis paralysis is mesmerizing. *Unsettled Disruption* is a highly recommended book for anyone who is trying to change paradigms and venture into doing something great."

—**Julian Torres**, Cofounder at Ontop (YCW21), Founder of Fitpal, Best-Selling Author of *La Estupidez Colectiva: Por qué usted tuvo esa idea primero y no es millonario*

"As the pace of change escalates, entrepreneurs and innovators need a proven approach for agile strategy development and frequent adaptation to implementation plans—the core. Juana-Catalina's career has provided her with a unique cross-industry perspective on streamlining the process for purpose-driven innovation. *Unsettled Disruption* is a must-read if you are serious about scaling social impact in an environment of uncertain conditions."

    —**Maurice L. Woods**, President and CEO, Easterseals South Florida

"*Unsettled Disruption* provides a practical framework for finding new ideas and defining core strategies to disrupt and create a new purposeful future. Highly recommended."

    —**Chuck Martin**, CEO, Net Future Institute, *NY Times* Business Best-Selling Author

"Juana's book *Unsettled Disruption* has a lot of relevance in the times we are living in. Purpose-driven innovations are three easy-to-pronounce words but very hard to practice and deliver. Fortunately, Juana's book makes the process easy to understand and administer. Right from the nuances to disruptive innovation, the frameworks, and the future, this book has it all and comes from the experience of a thought leader and provocateur. Reinventing strategies is a daunting task of unfreezing the status quo, running to the new horizon with innovations, and freezing the ways disruption changes businesses for the better. *Unsettled Disruption* would put you on a journey of understanding the disruptive innovation pathways better."

—**Rishi Kapal**, Former CXO of Fortune 500s, United Nations Speaker, Best-Selling Author of *Kites in a Hurricane* and *Managing Large Teams*

"Once every decade you come across a game-changing book. *Unsettled Disruption* is one of them. Juana-Catalina Rodriguez is introducing a new and solid framework on how to disrupt. The framework is applied to examples of both successes and failures of well-known companies. *Unsettled*

Disruption is a must-read for all executives and founders who want to fully understand disruption."

—**Raphaël Auwerkerken**, Millennial Entrepreneur and Angel Investor, Founder of Webgroup, Ifonix Innovations, Drawify, Proxico, ND Group

"Evolution is not about survival or reframing the old business model; it's about thriving on disruption. Companies are doing okay in incremental improvements but failing to adapt to the new changing ecosystem. Timely, relevant, and ready for use, Juana-Catalina's book encourages readers to rebuild their purpose-driven innovation journey from the start: meaning, framework, proven experience, and the future. This book delivers practical guidance with the firsthand experience of a thought leader."

—**Arijit Bhattacharyya**, Serial Entrepreneur, Technologist, Angel Investor, TEDx Speaker, Global VC, Government Advisor

"Companies get in serious trouble because they do not embrace change. In her great book, Juana-Catalina gives C-level and entrepreneurs a great framework to actively and systematically embrace change make it the next business success."

—**R. Paul Vuolle,** Managing Director, Bellevue SME Advisors, Best-Selling Author of *Lead Now, Manage Later*

"Outstanding. *Unsettled Disruption* is a priority #1 reading for any business manager who needs to navigate his/her business with foresight. Disruption is accelerating, and the provided practical and comprehensive *Unsettled Disruption* framework puts us in the driver seat!"

—**Claus Hirzmann**, Strategic Finance Founder

"We all need more disruption and bravery to do so. Juana's book gives us a wide array of actions and ideas to use and examples that show how the new world works. It is essential that we embrace this."

—**Marcus Kirsch,** Founder and Author of *The Wicked Company*

"Some start their business innovation journey by firstly calling for many ideas. In fact, many people assume that generating new ideas is the beginning of any business innovation funnel. Actually, that's not true. It is not the idea but the reason why you are looking for ideas that truly matters. If you are not solving a large enough problem that you could globally serve with a scalable solution, you are not running with the big idea. In *Unsettled Disruption*, Juana-Catalina Rodriguez reminds us that the very first step of any innovation journey is about what you stand for, not because of the ideas but because of the purpose you intend to pursue obsessively."

—**Hamilton Mann,** Group Director, Global Digital Marketing and Digital Transformation of Thales, Mentor with MIT IDEAS Social Innovation Challenge, MIT Priscilla King Gray (PKG) Center, Secretary General of No More Plastic

"Juana-Catalina has provided a structured and documented business framework in her new book *Unsettled Disruption*. With her insight, multiple examples, and explanations along with the method and process, reading this leaves you with a step-by-step process for being a disruptor and creating a whole new category yourselves. Let's start disrupting!"

—**Howard H Prager,** Leadership Consultant, Executive Coach, Author of *Make Someone's Day: Becoming a Memorable Leader in Work and Life*

UNSETTLED DISRUPTION

Step-by-Step Guide for **Harnessing the Evolving Path** of **Purpose-Driven Innovation**

JUANA-CATALINA RODRIGUEZ

Published by
Rupa Publications India Pvt. Ltd 2025
7/16, Ansari Road, Daryaganj
New Delhi 110002

Sales centres:
Bengaluru Chennai
Hyderabad Jaipur Kathmandu
Kolkata Mumbai Prayagraj

Copyright © Juana-Catalina Rodriguez 2025
Original English language edition published by Koehler Books 3705
Shore Drive, Virginia Beach Virginia 23455, USA
Arranged via Licensor's Agent: DropCap Inc.

The views and opinions expressed in this book are the author's
own and the facts are as reported by her which have been
verified to the extent possible, and the publishers are not in
any way liable for the same.

All rights reserved.
No part of this publication may be reproduced, transmitted,
or stored in a retrieval system, in any form or by any means, electronic,
mechanical, photocopying, recording or otherwise, without the prior
permission of the publisher.

P-ISBN: 978-93-5702-717-5
E-ISBN: 978-93-5702-764-9

First impression 2025

10 9 8 7 6 5 4 3 2 1

The moral right of the author has been asserted.

Printed in India

This book is sold subject to the condition that it shall not, by way of
trade or otherwise, be lent, resold, hired out, or otherwise circulated,
without the publisher's prior consent, in any form of binding or
cover other than that in which it is published.

To my son—love, energy, and smiles that make my inspiration flourish.
To my husband, who empowers me across all my writing journey.
To Luke, our dog who was staring at me every day, forcing me to take a daily dose of fresh air.
And, to you. To all the entrepreneurs and innovators facing disruption challenges and looking for a path to build a purpose-driven future.

Juana-Catalina

CONTENTS

Why Should You Read *Unsettled Disruption*? 1

PART I: WHAT AND WHY

Chapter 1: Disruptive Innovation is Changing
the Face of Business Strategies 11

Chapter 2: The Immediate Need of Getting
Disruptive Innovation Right 21

PART II: THE FRAMEWORK

Chapter 3: The Framework Overview......................................31

Chapter 4: Disruption Trends...42

Chapter 5: How to Assess Your Industry..................................52

Chapter 6: Honing in on Jobs-to-be-Done..............................64

Chapter 7: Five Most Common Jobs-to-be-Done Challenges......77

Chapter 8: The "How" Behind Value Chain Disruption............85

Chapter 9: Business Model Innovation...................................96

Chapter 10: Technology as Disruption Enabler......................110

PART III: PROVEN EXPERIENCE

Chapter 11: Incumbents Came out Stronger via Self-Disruption......121

Chapter 12: New Disruptors' Generation..............................127

Chapter 13: Lessons from Companies
That Failed to Handle Disruption 137

Chapter 14: 2020 Disruptors 143

PART IV: THE FUTURE

Chapter 15: How Purpose Can Harness Disruption................161

Chapter 16: The Road to Unsettled Disruption,
Given David and Goliath 174

Connecting the *Unsettled Disruption* Dots...........................178

Acknowledgments 188

About the Author 191

References 193

WHY SHOULD YOU READ *UNSETTLED DISRUPTION*?

LET'S START WITH A question: Why do some companies not see disruption coming while others harness the power of disruptive innovation?

It was the end of 2017, and I was reading about the Toys-R-Us bankruptcy [1]. I remember my first visit to a Toys-R-Us store back in the '90s, with their impressive product endcaps, massive inventory, and spectrum of merchandise. In the end, nostalgia couldn't save them. The once-mighty retailer struggled to keep up with changing consumer trends, environment, and technology.

Like Toys-R-Us, Blockbuster, and Borders Bookstores, and many other entrepreneurs, we see more companies missing the disruptive innovation opportunity while others thrive in an environment of unsettled disruption.

Most recently, and just a few days after the first pandemic lockdown, I got a call from Mark. He was frustrated as he had worked for the last year to develop his startup project to improve farmers' production by leveraging internet of things technology to help them save time and money. He just launched in January 2020, but everything was suddenly stopped.

There was a touch of mixed feelings as Mark was also thankful to be safe at home with his family in these uncertain times. During the first two weeks of the lockdown, Mark was dumbstruck. As a founder, he felt very lonely and worried about finances as he had invested almost all his savings in this new venture.

Then after two months of lockdown, he took time to reflect and look into the future. He sounds like a different person, learning and accepting that it will be a while before things get back to normal. But this was an excellent opportunity for his company when he realized that digitalization would be a significant milestone in the coming months. He decided to adapt and reinvent his business. "Juana, this is not going to be easy, but I need to do something and work my way out of this crisis to make it happen," he beamed from the other side of our online meeting.

As intra- or entrepreneurs, we are always worried about innovation, scaling up, reframing our business model, and getting new customers. I have been working with several entrepreneurs, organizations, and companies struggling and even facing an existential business crisis. They wonder if their idea is still relevant in the current scenario and and if they will be able to linger on if the situation continues for an unforeseeable future. This new situation caught us off guard.

The disruption caused by the COVID-19 pandemic is incomparable. Overnight, entire businesses, education systems, and health infrastructures came to a knockout of our world's interconnectedness and the vulnerability that comes with it. Many sectors, such as fashion, sports, tourism, and brick-and-mortar retailers, faced unprecedented mass closures and witnessed monumental layoffs. Even "unicorns" like Airbnb fired more than 1,900 people in one month [2], and the airline industry encountered the same fate with massive layoffs over 2020 [3].

With far-reaching physical lockdowns across the world an ever-present reality, the question arises of developing new systems and economies that possess the resilience needed to thrive under uncertain conditions.

We can't predict how businesses will evolve. Still, we know that most organizations focus on identifying and capitalizing on new opportunities created by the changing landscape.

According to the McKinsey Global Innovation survey, more than 84 percent [4] of executives agree that innovation is important to growth strategy. Today, they are looking for new, innovative ideas to sustain or scale their business, as they cannot operate as they have in the past.

Nowadays, entrepreneurs, innovators, and companies face the test of redefining their strategy in a short time frame. They are under immense pressure to innovate and transform their business models, operations, and products to make them more compelling and competitive in the challenging marketplace.

In 2020 and more than ever, we learned that what made a company successful historically may no longer be possible during or after a global crisis.

WHY IS DISRUPTIVE INNOVATION CRITICAL?

It's not just about the rapid changes occurring worldwide, but also the new way we do and understand business. Those changes are going to continue to speed up. That's why it's being coined "the exponential age" [5] because commerce and innovation will get exponentially faster.

Several transformation projects and business digitalization catapulted from years of hesitation into mere weeks of implementation during the pandemic. Video conferencing company Zoom's daily users increased thirty times in just four months, with daily meeting users reaching upwards of 300 million in April 2020 [6]. Zoom is now worth more than the seven largest airline companies. [7]

In April 2020, educational institutions closed in 195 countries, affecting more than 1.3 billion students [8]. Millions of students shifted from in-person classes to virtual online classrooms, and EdTech became a priority for investors. Elon Musk, CEO of SpaceX, claims that human life on other planets is a critical step in the evolution of humanity. He is planning to expand the earth's reach to other planets in our solar system, anticipating 2026 as the year of first travel to Mars [9].

While there are thousands of these examples available, a TikTok executive said it best during a 2020 web summit: "You will get disrupted if you don't disrupt." [10] Many companies are not only looking to what's next, but overall how to get to what's next.

HOW DO YOU APPROACH DISRUPTIVE INNOVATION?

Many organizations and innovators struggle to survive and tend to forget that looking ahead is better than simply studying the past. A new strategic approach is the only solution to this economic pressure and consumer's rapid speed. These days, we speak about "disruptive innovation" and discuss success stories and failures, but you may still wonder, "How do I start? Where do I find disruptive ideas?"

The definition of insanity attributed to Albert Einstein is doing the same thing over and over, expecting a different result. If you want unsettled disruption, you need to change the paradigm. Creativity doesn't always switch on like a lightbulb in our heads. It requires a better understanding of the problem you want to solve and the factors that create the problem. It requires a framework and the vision to define the next steps to advance towards the future.

There is no magic formula for the coming years. Still, there is evidence through experience that a systematic process helps you to connect the dots and create your disruptive innovation strategy.

WHAT WILL YOU LEARN FROM THIS BOOK?

The motivation of this book comes from a desire to give you the means to achieve unsettled disruption. This is a step-by-step framework to define your strategy of becoming a disrupter and/or learning how to avoid being disrupted.

This practical guide combines the concepts, tools, examples, and proven business stories to ensure that you can distinguish between developments that will last and drive change versus those that will fade away from our evolving world. The process developed and supporting examples that follow will help you to unfold disruption strategies and understand the mechanisms that made disruption happen.

Unsettled Disruption will help you uncover why companies are being disrupted, how to identify the disruption potential in your industry, and how disruptors find innovative ideas to serve unattended customers.

In the first part of this book, we explain what disruptive innovation is, and why you need to get disruptive innovation right.

The second part reflects on the mechanisms that make a disruption possible at three levels:

External—considers the external trends and assesses the chances of disruption in an industry.

Core—includes the four elements that make disruption possible, job-to-be-done, value chain, business model, and technology.

Strategic Purpose—entails the core elements of your business's mission and the strategic orientation, the "why."

Readers will learn from proven experience how incumbents came out stronger through self-disruption; you will understand the new wave of disruptors, and learn from companies that failed to handle disruption as well as from disruptors that flourished during the 2020 pandemic.

To get the most relevant and practical information, we included stories from my personal experiences and my research of companies like Netflix, Dollar Shave Club, Airbnb, Sony, Ferrero, Starbucks, Western Union, Kodak, Dell, IKEA, Getaround, Twitter, Spotify, Alibaba, Tesla, Amazon, Apple, Google, Atari, Mars, Hilti, Easy Bank, eBay, Skype, Wikipedia, Microsoft, LEGO, Disney, Warby Parker, Canva, Blockbuster, Nokia, Toys-R-Us, Borders, Seventh Generation, Patagonia, Tala, Ben & Jerry's, Zoom, TikTok, Slack and Vigga.

WHO IS THIS BOOK FOR?

This book is for those who are looking for new ideas, who seek to create long-lasting success and believe that change requires others' collaboration. For those who want to unfold disruptive innovation to create a new and purposeful future, *Unsettled Disruption* offers you a path to harness the power of disruptive innovation.

Unsettled Disruption is written for passionate innovators working inside large organizations, medium-sized companies, as well as entrepreneurs looking for new opportunities. It is for those who understand the *why*, but still need guidance with the *what* and the *how*.

If you are a business leader, C-Suite, or high-level executive responsible for driving innovation, this book will give you the strategic guidance and inspiration to drive your team to start their disruptive innovation journey.

My mission is to inspire you to unlock the full potential of your own disruption. I want to give you the tools and techniques to face the years ahead with a clear purpose of making a better world because you have more power than you realize.

WHO IS THE AUTHOR?

During the last twenty years, I have been actively helping entrepreneurs and organizations harness disruptive innovation's power. I went deep into my research and had the opportunity to join the Stanford GSB LEAD community, where I found the missing pieces of the puzzle.

My professional experience has allowed me to understand the urgency of providing a framework that helps innovators identify different opportunities. I started this journey with a plethora of questions, such as:

1. How do disruptors keep track of new trends and demands?
2. What are the ways to identify disruption potential in an industry?

3. How do businesses identify what customer requirements are unfulfilled today?
4. Which is the most unsatisfied customer segment of the industry?
5. How do disruptors find innovative ideas to serve the unattended customer segment better than incumbents?
6. How do they deliver this new value?
7. How do they define their innovative business models?

By answering these questions, I have identified a framework to help you to start your own unsettled disruption journey.

LET'S START THIS JOURNEY

Clayton Christensen, the father of disruptive innovation, is one of the principal sources of inspiration for this book. Thanks to his fantastic work, we experienced a better understanding of this concept.

Charles Darwin noted, "It is not the strongest species that survive, nor the most intelligent, but the ones most responsive to change." Author Andy Grove said, "There are two options: adapt or die." And many other bright minds remind us of the need to change and evolve.

Hence, we're living in changing times, and those companies that lag behind will become as extinct as the dinosaurs. To those who have an open mind, who wish to discover the road to innovation, and believe that a process will help you drive these great ideas, I offer you a path.

Let's walk together and start harnessing the power of disruptive innovation and build towards a purpose-driven future.

PART I
WHAT AND WHY

PART I
WHAT AND WHY

CHAPTER 1
DISRUPTIVE INNOVATION IS CHANGING THE FACE OF BUSINESS STRATEGIES

"Minds are like parachutes; they work best when open."
Thomas Dewar

BEFORE THE PANDEMIC, WE moved to a new region with many hopes and expectations for my husband's new job. During his job interviews in November 2019, he got many insights into how the airline industry was booming. The company looking to hire him had a considerable challenge to optimize manufacturing as they have orders guaranteed until 2026. But in March 2020, orders started to get canceled, and management began to get stressed. As I am writing this book, instead of dealing with growth, they are now dealing with restructuring, layoffs, and capacity optimization to keep the company alive.

Would they be available to disrupt themselves?

In the current times, many companies face the test of reinventing their strategy in a very short time frame, not even weeks but days. This redefinition had become the only solution to the environment and economic pressure, and the way the consumer has started to think.

A strategic way to move forward is to understand disruptive innovation as the first step to better determine a new strategy, and how, by scanning different opportunities, to be available to set the path to what's next. For doing so, we will start the unsettled disruption journey by describing what disruptive innovation is.

Before moving forward, let's clarify two terms that will be used in this book quite often: "incumbents" and "new entrants" [11].

Incumbent is an existing company with an established position in an industry. The company possesses market share, an established brand, and business relationships with suppliers. The incumbent strategy may be to self-disrupt to prevent disruption from new entrants, as Microsoft or Disney did.

New entrant is a new company that enters an industry in which it did not previously operate. In this industry, the company seeks to establish itself by competing for customers and resources. The new entrant may disrupt the industry it enters. In this category, we can mention companies like Netflix, Airbnb, or Warby Parker, who disrupted the entertainment, hospitality and eyewear industry.

WHAT IS DISRUPTIVE INNOVATION?

The term "disruptive innovation" [12] coined by Clayton Christensen [13], describes a process by which a product or service takes root initially in simple applications at the bottom of a market, and then relentlessly moves upmarket, eventually displacing established business referred to as "incumbents."

Disruptive innovation begins with a small company entering the low-end market or creating a new segment. Then they move upmarket and challenge established businesses. They focus on a segment ignored by the incumbents, and offer the most cost-effective, accessible, and straightforward product. The following chapters will explain how companies like Netflix, Airbnb, Warby Parker, and others have come this way to disrupt industries.

As incumbents focus on improving their products and services for their most demanding customers, they usually exceed these segments' needs and ignore other segments' expectations. Some corporations tell their teams to focus on the most significant "big customers," but have a hard time being profitable with the small ones. When they finally realize this small/medium size segment's potential, they create new programs and hire business development teams to launch their offers, even if their solutions don't answer these segments' requirements. They get stuck with higher prices, not-needed features, or even unmatched business models [14].

We have seen in the market several examples of these unwanted features in the *Forbes* article "Are Most Of Your Product's Features . . . Useless?" [15]. Here Tom Taulli mentions that 80 percent of the typical cloud software product features are rarely or never used. Another example, just check your car's fancy features; we don't even know how many we have used as social media integration [16].

Instead, new entrants create disruption by targeting overlooked segments, gaining a footprint by delivering proper functionality at a lower price. As incumbents initially ignore these segments, new entrants move upmarket, improving their performance that mainstream customers require, but presenting their advantages. This drives new entrants' success and displaces incumbents.

Christensen explained that disruptive innovations are not necessarily breakthrough innovations that dramatically alter how business is done. However, they do consist of solutions that are simple to acquire and affordable at the least. Disruptors such as Airbnb, Netflix, Zoom, Skype, and Slack started with products and services that appear modest at their outset but have the potential to transform an industry.

In the case of Airbnb, they started in the low-end market by renting mattresses in San Francisco using a low-cost prototype of their platform. Their customers were users who couldn't afford a hotel. At that time, incumbent hotel chains didn't see the offer as a threat.

With time, Airbnb improved its value by leveraging technology to provide a better service, and increased its guest and host reach, to become attractive for the incumbent's core customers. Airbnb disrupted the hospitality industry. Nowadays, even companies such as Marriot are shifting into the

Airbnb model [17]. The distinctive difference is that disruptive innovations supersede existing processes to redefine the industry standards.

In Figure 1, we can see how Clayton Christensen illustrated this concept [14]. New entrants start in the lower end of the market with a lower performance offer. At the same time, established firms keep their trajectory of sustaining innovations but adding new features, improving the current offer without questioning the status quo or seeing the new entrants as a threat. In the beginning, mainstream customers are not interested in new entrants offering lower quality and value. But as new entrants evolve with competitive business models and offers, they start to grab the mainstream market from incumbents. Just think how Zoom started serving small and medium companies, and then evolved into helping large organizations in a few years.

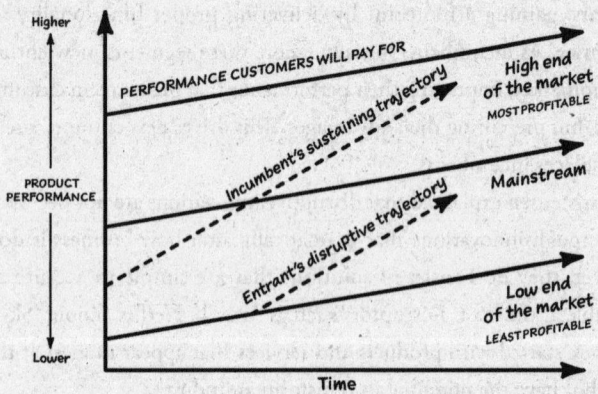

Figure 1 - What is Disruptive Innovation? - Clayton Christensen HBR.ORG

Understanding disruptive innovation will empower intrapreneurs, entrepreneurs, or aspiring entrepreneurs to seek opportunities to disrupt industries, and change their venture or company's status quo.

- Disruptive innovation is when a product or service initially takes in simple applications and evolves over time. It does not target incumbents' mainstream customers until the offerings reach or exceed their standards.
- Disruptive innovation is typically designed to be less expensive and more accessible by creating a new business model targeting the low-end market or a specific niche segment overlooked by incumbents.
- Disruptive innovation is not just about technology. It combines strategic enablers, including market fit, user experience, value chain, business model innovation, and technology.
- Disruptive innovation is hard to see coming and isn't taken seriously by the incumbent, but the mix can eventually displace established players.

Now, let me illustrate the disruptive innovation definition with a couple of examples.

DOLLAR SHAVE CLUB DISRUPTED MEN'S SHAVING EXPERIENCE

Dollar Shave Club ("DSC") [18] is an American company that delivers razors and other personal grooming products to customers by mail every month. DSC was launched in 2011 and successfully disrupted men's traditional shaving experience by offering a new solution to the customer's basic needs.

After three years down the road, Dollar Shave Club claimed 48 percent of the online razor market [19], shaking up conventional leaders as Gillette and Schick. By May 2019, the company has grown to include over 600 employees globally, and has more than 4 million subscribers [20]. In July 2016, Unilever acquired Dollar Shave in an all-cash $1 billion deal [21].

The salient features of their disruptive model include:

- Disruption is a process where a service initially takes root in simple applications in the low-end market. DSC identified "a job to be done" in a specific segment by providing an affordable solution to a real, relatable problem shared by men (and even women). Instead of paying a minimum of $20 a month, they now paid just $4 a month—groundbreaking, right?
- Dollar Shave Club disrupted the value chain mold by creating an online platform and delivering the product directly to the consumer instead of going through the local store.
- They also leveraged technology and internet penetration to develop their value proposition, launch this new subscription model, and use data to improve their offer and explore new opportunities that create even more value for their customers.
- This unique customer experience was transformed into a monthly "delight." DSC offered a new value around the product that customers didn't know they wanted or could ask for. It became a user experience disrupted model. As described on the DSC website, "With DSC you'll have quality generic alternatives automatically delivered to your door for as little as $4.00 a month. No contracts, no hidden fees [22]."

The razor industry is known for spending tens of millions of dollars a year on research and development. DSC co-founder Michael Dubin mocked the incumbent's practices in his launch video [23] by asking users: "Do you like spending $20 a month on brand-name razors? Stop paying for shave tech you don't need."

For decades, Gillette was essentially alone, with just its lackluster drugstore aisle competitor Schick. So, in the beginning, these competitors didn't heed much to the DSC model. However, Dollar Shave Club took the core of their business. Then, it was too late for them to catch up. Incumbents were stuck on their traditional "known" model.

Gillette, the major incumbent, was forced to react by reducing prices, launching a shave club of its own, and even venturing. It wasn't just about mega-innovative razors. Dollar Shave Club made a point by criticizing flaws in the existing business model of conventional men's shaving products and purchase experience. This is disruption.

NETFLIX SELF-DISRUPTION PROCESS

Netflix started in 1997 as a DVD distribution company that had to compete with Blockbuster back in the day when it was the leading company that rented DVDs [24]. Netflix was dealing with a competitor that was extremely popular and renowned. Then, Netflix grew its subscriber base by offering free trials and other deals that made convenient rental services popular.

In 2020, Netflix's annual revenue rose to $24.9 billion, a 24.01 percent increase year-over-year [25], and by the end of 2020, Netflix had over 200 million users [26]. As of March 2021, they had grown a market value of $223.5 billion [27]. This impressive growth demonstrates that Netflix successfully disrupted not only incumbents but itself without being displaced.

The salient features of their disruptive model include:

- Most innovations begin as small-scale experiments. Thus, Netflix started in the '90s as a movie-rental service by email. Netflix then chose the path of technology and online viewing, a significant disruption in its business strategy. If Netflix had not eventually begun to serve a broader segment of the market, Blockbuster's decision to ignore this competitor would not have been a strategic blunder [28].
- As defined by Clayton Christensen [14], disruptive innovation occurs when a new entrant overlooks segments with a new offering (and often a new business model). This disruption is what Netflix did to Blockbuster by coming up with a less expensive, simple, and accessible model. Its original mail order service didn't provide the instant gratification that Blockbuster did, but it was far more

straightforward and less costly (as users were tired of having to pay painful late fees).
- The Netflix model then evolved thanks to technology by moving from DVD delivery to streaming, even if it underperformed in the beginning. It was still simpler, faster, and less costly, and attractive to new users and existing users who were over-served by the DVD business.
- The technology was the real game-changer in this scenario as the internet, mobile phone, and streaming allowed Netflix to shift to streaming video over the internet, making their business model a more comprehensive selection of content to its monthly subscribers at a fixed cost.

At the time of writing this book, Netflix is one of the rare companies benefiting from the global pandemic. [29] Netflix added 15.8 million subscribers in the first quarter of 2020, more than double the 7.2 million expected. Their growth has been more than 22 percent year over year. This is disruption.

AN OVERNIGHT SUCCESS

In his blog, Seth Godin [30] said, "It takes about six years to become an overnight success." Mark Zuckerberg's Facebook took seven years to become a cash flow optimistic company, and Bill Gates took eleven years to land his first big deal with IBM.

For some incumbents, the belief is that to explore and exploit new disruptive models companies should create a separate division that operates under the protection of senior leadership. This model has worked in some cases, but it is a painfully slow process that may not provide the desired results.

However, in a face-off between the disruption model and traditional incumbents, this is the time where disruptors have a slight edge: in this new era, responses, products, and services are required instantly by most users. This trend has accelerated during the pandemic, as business models and strategies have faced a disruption themselves. Zoom, Slack, and Netflix are only a few examples of this argument.

TAKEAWAYS

Keeping in mind the examples explained above, let's reflect on our five takeaways about disruptive innovation definition.

- It is a process by which a product or service initially takes in simple applications.
- It is typically designed to be less expensive and more accessible by creating a new business model targeting the low-end market or a niche segment.
- It is hard to see coming and isn't taken seriously by the incumbent.
- It is not just about technology. It combines strategic enablers including market fit, user experience, value chain, business model innovation, and technology.
- This mix can eventually displace established players known as incumbents.

Entrepreneurs are often the ones that develop new products or services to revolutionize an entire industry. They can start small in a niche market and then scale the product to appeal to a broader group of people. They don't necessarily need to be intimidated by bigger players either, because established companies are probably not interested in developing these low-margin products or solutions.

We still have a lot to learn about "disruptive innovation" for running a new business. Its definition is evolving as new players enter the market within the context of an exponential revolution and uncertain encounters.

On the other hand, the reality is that a better understanding of disruption and learning from others' experiences can help us to define our position as entrepreneurs or intrapreneurs. The understanding demonstrates that a systematic framework helps to kick off and accelerate the disruptive innovation process. *Unsettled Disruption* gives an actionable path and tools to harness this strategy.

Now, as evident as it sounds, let's explore some of the reasons why we need to get disruptive innovation right.

CHAPTER 2
THE IMMEDIATE NEED OF GETTING DISRUPTIVE INNOVATION RIGHT

"If you allow the fear of failure to become a barrier, you're already putting roadblocks in your way."
Richard Branson

IT WAS THE LATE '90s; I was working in a company that was the market leader of French fries across all regions, selling our products to big chains like McDonald's, Burger King, and Wendy's. We got around 80 percent of supermarket shelf space. Our position was very comfortable, and frozen French fries represented 95 percent of our business. I had recently been named marketing director of the Andean region.

The regional CEO came, very worried, to my office that morning. He'd had a discussion with a sales guy who mentioned a new entrant in the restaurant segment, an emerging brand offering low-cost products, lower quality, and better prices. He asked me what to do.

I told him that I wasn't worried. We were the market leader, and our quality and brand were well-positioned. He looked at me with no judgment and said, "Maybe we don't have the right offer for these customers." Then he said, "Let's do a quick test, pack some products, and build a new reference with different standards—French fries with various sizes, transparent packaging, deliveries just once a week, and branded differently."

I was astonished. In only five minutes he did what was supposed to be my job. Of course, it wasn't in five minutes. He had fifteen years of experience in the field and a passion for keeping eyes open on customer trends.

Indeed, this offer was a success. It grabbed 20 percent of our sales, as we now answered an unserved market. One of my first lessons was to keep my eyes open to challenge our own business and watch out for any potential customer job-to-be-done.

Disruptive innovation has been changing business structures for several years now. Its core idea is the emergence of new businesses dedicated to serving a portion of the unanswered market. Thereby, disrupters start by offering new solutions to the segment not extensively attended before. They do not directly challenge the market leaders' presence, but they gradually redress the industry's business model. Remember, all innovators might not be disruptors, but all disruptors certainly are innovators.

For established businesses to compete with the disruptors, it is essential to identify them correctly in the first place. It will help them devise the right policies to beat the emerging powers and mold the current business structure to meet future challenges.

Richard Branson, founder of Virgin Group [31], explains how taking risks, acting upon your instinct, and shunning the conventional methods form the foundations of disruption. Companies like Netflix, Airbnb, and iTunes show us the disruptor's path by entering a new market, fulfilling particular demands instead of directly challenging the existing market leaders. But they weren't an overnight success. It was their systematic approach that made it happen.

For instance, Airbnb boosted the tourism industry by giving travelers a convenient and cheaper way to stay at a foreign destination. On the other side, Netflix and iTunes solutions changed the entertainment and music industries' future.

Therefore, if you want to benefit from disruptive innovation rather than being washed out, you need to understand the steps and tools that will help you to get it right. Overlooking disruptive innovation influence has and will only lead to a substantial reduction in market share, thereby affecting profits and the overall business in the mid- and long run.

Nevertheless, some incumbents, entrepreneurs, and even startups still do not take this concept seriously. Let's look at the stories of companies like Toys-R-Us, Kodak, or Blockbuster that overlooked disruptive innovation. With that said, here are five main reasons why leaders need a thorough understanding of disruptive innovation and why they should not overlook it.

1. DISRUPTIVE INNOVATION IS A GRADUAL PROCESS

Disruptors usually (not always) start as small-scale businesses to experiment with their ideas and develop successful working models. This evolving process enables them to offer better solutions to the existing problems left unanswered by established companies. Since they may challenge the business structure rather than just the product or particular service, disruptors shake the whole industry with new business models.

Making such a significant impact in a well-established industry cannot be done overnight. It takes several years. Take the example of the first discount department store in the '70s that opened around fifty years ago, such as Costco or Target. Despite those stores' establishment, the retailers were still using the conventional department store's model, born between 1900 and 1940, including Macy's or Galeries Lafayette [32]. That's because adopting an entirely new model would require excessive inputs and a substantial cut in profit. Moreover, since the new model already had a leader, competing would not be easy.

In any case, ignoring disruptors is not the best decision. That being so, it won't be possible if you have the right understanding of disruption.

2. DISRUPTIVE INNOVATION CAN BE DIFFICULT TO ANTICIPATE

With unpredictable technological developments, new consumer habits, and the need to survive in today's rapidly changing world, anticipating disruption can be challenging for some businesses.

Moreover, since disruptors do not focus on serving the incumbents' customers, they initially do not feel jeopardized. For example, Airbnb [33] started by serving budget travelers with the cheaper lodgings they sought during their trips, instead of shelling out their cash on expensive hotels. Such a service would not attract a five-star hotel's customers because initially, the low-cost Airbnb quarters were nothing compared to the quality of service of big-brand hotels.

It is one of the significant reasons why market leaders do not pay much attention to the new entrant. They are not attracting the incumbent's customers, and their offers are not seen as very competitive at the beginning of their road. However, things start to get out of hand when disruptors like Airbnb begin attracting the incumbents' loyal customers with a robust offer.

Hence, every business leader must anticipate the industry's disruptors to sustain their business and keep an eye on what is happening in the environment. For doing so, there are several tools that we will explore in *Unsettled Disruption*.

3. SNATCHES AWAY THE HARD-EARNED MARKET SHARE

Since Airbnb offers exceptionally affordable lodging charges [34], it has helped control the hotel rates. Although it did not affect hotels' regular high-paying customers, it substantially cut down on hotels' seasoned profits. Midtown Manhattan, one of the most significant examples, charged exceptionally high prices on New Year's Eve due to increased demand. Industry dynamics have changed since then.

Due to the proper use of advanced technology accompanied by an innovative business model, Airbnb could excel in its value to millions of travelers worldwide. Their service was mainly spread by word of mouth, which increased its credibility, enabling it to capitalize on their reputation.

Our research shows how disruption emerges from a combination of market demand, value chain analysis, business model innovation, and technology. This solid combo does not take long to throw incumbents off their thrones.

4. DISRUPTORS BRING NOVEL BUSINESS MODELS

Sony stands to be one of the victims of disruption. It was the first brand that made listening to music while walking possible through its Walkman [35]. However, it required the users to carry the cassettes along with the device.

That marked the start of music digitalization. After the Walkman, we had CD players that were much easier to carry. Moving on, we got MP3 players that further eased our pain, enabling us to carry our whole music studio in a pocket—what a dream for people born in the '70s and '80s.

Then, what disrupted Sony's Walkman and the music industry as a whole was Apple's iPod. It was much more portable and user-friendly. Moreover, you could store thousands of songs on one device.

On the other hand, it was not only about technology; the main factor that made Apple a disruptor is how it changed the music industry through this combination of exceptional customer experience and value chain disruption, "1000 songs in your pocket."

At the same time, Apple launched iTunes, which enabled the users to access any music they wanted. Since having to enjoy any music from around the world with just the click of a finger was something customers could have only dreamed of, it took Apple over the boundaries of the music industry.

What added even more value to the iPod was the legality of iTunes. Because of this, users could peacefully enjoy their music. Apple iPod would go on to hold a 78 percent market share from 2003 to 2011 in global MP3 players, with 300 million iPods sold in 10 years [36]. It was an innovative way to disrupt an industry with a new and proven business model.

5. DISRUPTIVE INNOVATION CAN AFFECT THE CURRENT CASH FLOW

Often, companies overlook new customer-driven products or services with the idea of keeping their current cash flow unharmed.

THINX's CEO, Miki Agarwal [37], founder of several social enterprises, has been working to break the taboo surrounding menstruation in developing countries. According to the UN's report, girls who do not have access to menstrual products do not leave their houses during menstruation [38], not to mention the health risks.

Her idea of providing absorbent underwear could have helped these women in the developing world, but the $15 billion tampon industry did not plan to change [37]. It feared losing its demand for tampons with the launch of the new product. Today, the market is moving in this direction, so this is a clear sign of another industry that is going to be disrupted by less expensive and more accessible solutions.

Let's move now to another sector and speak about Microsoft. It introduced the first consumer-operated operating system (OS). Since its OS was the only one in the market, people were forced to pay for it. It didn't plan on introducing smarter devices and operating systems for the sake of protecting its current financial position. However, it all changed when Apple stepped into the market, bringing innovative OS and user-friendly computing devices. Then, Google was set on the same mission of taking away the throne from Apple. But Microsoft's story didn't end here; we will explore later how this incumbent has succeeded by going into self-disruption.

TAKEAWAYS

Disruptive innovation has been changing business structures for several years now. Its core idea is the emergence of new businesses dedicated to serving a portion of an unanswered market. Thereby, disrupters start by offering new solutions to this segment not extensively attended before.

They do not directly challenge the market leaders' presence, but they gradually redress the industry's business model.

For established businesses to compete with the disruptors, they need to identify the disruptors correctly in the first place. This will help them devise the right policies to beat the emerging powers and mold the current business structure to meet future challenges.

Why?

- Disruptive innovation is a gradual process and usually starts as small-scale experiment.
- It can be challenging to anticipate, so we need to keep our eyes open to external and internal factors and trends.
- It can affect the cash flow, as a new entrant brings an innovative business model and changes the industry.
- It snatches away market share, including unserved and current customers, as the value chain structure can change.

The term "disruptive innovation" might confuse or make companies afraid unless they understand its definition. It is essential to know whether it was a clear-cutting edge innovation or disruption. It is not always necessary for an innovation to be disruptive, but disruption is always about innovation.

Therefore, businesses must learn how to use unsettled disruption and identify new opportunities to define their strategy. You will now dive into the second part of this book that describes step-by-step how to analyze the pillars that will help you connect the dots and define your disruption strategy, the unsettled disruption framework.

PART II
THE FRAMEWORK

CHAPTER 3
THE FRAMEWORK OVERVIEW

"The world, as we have created it, is a process of our thinking. It cannot be changed without changing our thinking."
Albert Einstein

THE ABILITY TO IDENTIFY new opportunities does not always come like a lightbulb of creativity switching on in our heads. Instead, it is a combination of experience gained through discussions, analysis, and other such means that makes us creative. It requires connecting the dots and integrating the essential elements responsible for forming a new disruptive path.

I remember the day in 2013 when we were attending a retailers' event in Paris, presenting our latest innovation—the Personal Smart Shopper—a system of automated brick-and-mortar stores. At that time, Amazon Go was nowhere in the picture. In fact, many retailers were considering developing mobile applications for their stores, but at that moment, it did not achieve the importance of a core business.

One of the biggest reasons was that underdeveloped mobile applications made online payments questionable. Telecom operators and banks were still trying to figure out the formation of an integrated mobile payment system, the business model, and how to get the right user experience.

Many visitors stopped by our stand to check out and even test our system, designed to allow people to scan their products, and checkout and pay via their mobile phones. The idea was to form an integrated omnichannel retail strategy—blending physical and digital retail experience. We used NFC tags to offer an Amazon-like experience: "If you buy this, you would like that."

At the event, a visitor came to us to appreciate our creativity while also questioning our system, saying retailers might not be ready to disrupt their system and introduce an automated store. He asked us where this idea came from. I smiled and replied that our team had been working on it for eight months. We had interviewed many retailers, conducted discussions with users and different stakeholders, analyzed market trends, and evaluated the ecosystem. Only after that were we finally able to come up with several ideas that were being prototyped and tested. Our automated store offered a seamless user experience while challenging the retail value chain from start to end through the proper use of technology, IoT (Internet of things), mobile devices, and connectivity.

SO, WHY DO WE NEED A SYSTEMATIC PROCESS?

While working with several entrepreneurs, intrapreneurs, and innovators in the past years, I realized that a systematic process is extremely helpful to connect the dots to identify potential sources of disruption and define a clear strategic path.

Large organizations that are continually being disrupted have accepted that their existing business strategies, structures, and techniques may no longer be valid. They are powerful enough to beat new entrants backed by resources and advanced technology but lose track on the disruption potential by focusing on their traditional models.

There is an urgency to understand how to define a path towards disruptive innovation. Today, the "exponential revolution," the pandemic, and the need for sustainability have accelerated this need to change.

Considering such worsening situations, some organizations are promoting innovation by arranging hackathons and innovative workshops. But all they do is create innovation initiatives without significant outcomes. Such innovation activities are only meant to create hype about a possible planned innovation which does not have an impact on a practical basis.

Disruptive innovation is far more than that. Over time, the disruption concept has evolved from being just a change in technology or sales channel to a powerful mix of all forces that are coercively changing the business world. We need to clear away these made-up narratives and dive deeper into the details to unravel the realities of disruption.

Companies struggling to survive in the market often forget that they need to look forward to move ahead. Their forgetfulness towards this fact prevents their progress, and they continue to look backward. Disruption is not an overnight success. It requires a step-by-step approach to focus our efforts to reach the potentially disruptive territory we intend to conquer. Let's unravel this process.

INNOVATOR VS. DISRUPTOR

To define a strategy to disrupt an industry or protect a business from external disruption, we need first to recall the difference between an innovator and a disruptor.

An innovator—introduces a new product, service, idea, or methodology.

A disruptor—someone who substantially changes the working model of an industry.

Launching a new product or service only—no matter how technologically advanced—will not be marked as disruption. Newer goods and services are only innovations when they do not mingle with the structure of an industry. An example of this is when Gillette was investing millions in improving razors without changing the industry structure but instead focused on better razors. This is called "incremental innovation." It is about creative ideas that are continuously applied to existing products or services to improve them and provide more value to their current market.

It focuses on enhancing product-market fit and performance. It is done by using features like product line expansions, cost reductions, and next-generation products. Businesses with incremental innovation occur in the short term and create a relatively smaller impact on the market.

On the other hand, disruption shakes the entire industry's structure, altering the ways incumbents serve their existing customers. Disruptors like Dollar Shave Club, Netflix, or Airbnb target the untapped audience of a market and create value for them in terms of quality, experience, functionality, price, etc. These audiences are known as new customer segments.

THE UNSETTLED DISRUPTION FRAMEWORK

The unsettled disruption framework explains how a business can redefine new value for a particular customer segment and eventually disrupt the industry. We have seen that disruptors target new customer segments with new value propositions, and the questions arise:

1. How do disruptors keep track of new trends and demands?
2. What are the ways to identify disruption potential in an industry?
3. How do businesses identify which customer requirements are unfulfilled today?
4. Which is the most unsatisfied customer segment of the industry?
5. How do disruptors find innovative ideas to serve the unattended customer segment better than incumbents?
6. How do they deliver this new value?
7. How do they define their innovative business models?

Answering these questions is the focus of this framework. A systematic process is required to uncover the specific mechanisms that make a disruption possible. At first glance, the framework comprises three levels for identifying un-tapped disruption.

External—considers the external trends and assesses the chances of disruption in an industry.

Core—includes the four elements that make disruption possible, job-to-be-done, value chain, business model, and technology.

Strategic Purpose—entails the core elements of your business's mission and the strategic orientation, the "why."

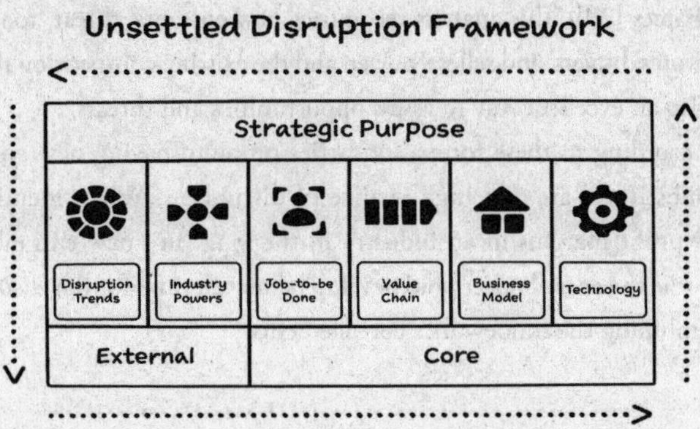

Unsettled Disruption Framework

Strategic Purpose					
Disruption Trends	Industry Powers	Job-to-be Done	Value Chain	Business Model	Technology
External		Core			

Figure 2 - Unsettled Disruption Framework

EXTERNAL FACTORS

This first level of the framework includes the external disruption trends and the need to assess the industry's powers to define the sector's chances of disruption.

DISRUPTION TRENDS

The first step is to look into the environment and systems to identify different disruption trends. There is an extensive list of macro sources of disruption to look for and learn to prepare for what could be the unexpected future. Ignoring them will leave even the biggest organizations vulnerable to disruption.

In Chapter 4, you will explore in detail each of them, including economics, education, geopolitics, demographics, environment, and other trends that could affect a company's core business in the long run. While planning for unsettled disruption, you must keep an eye on each trend and define how they impact your business.

PREDICT CHANCES OF DISRUPTION IN YOUR INDUSTRY

The second step is to predict how attractive the industry would be for disruptors. These chances of disruption can be foreseen using Porter's Five Forces [39]. This analysis recognizes new entrants' threat, room for substitutes, buyers' and sellers' power, and the existing competition rivalry. It is also an excellent way to assess opportunities and threats.

According to these forces, industries prone to having new entrants and substitutes are at a high chance of disruption. When identifying better profit margins in an industry in the long run, new entrants can overcome the entry barriers and develop better offerings for the customers by combining the framework's core elements.

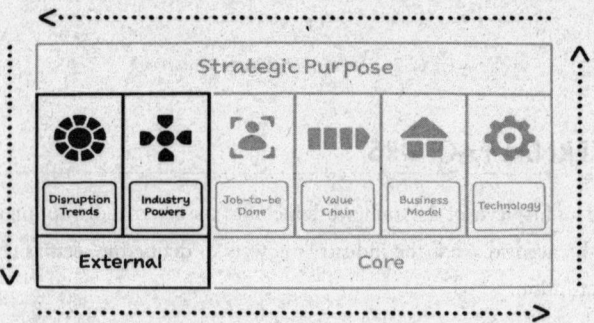

Figure 3 - Unsettled Disruption – External Factors

CORE PILLARS

The unsettled disruption framework's core includes the four pillars that, when combined, will make disruption happen: job-to-be-done, value chain, business model, and technology.

JOBS-TO-BE-DONE

Jobs-to-be-done focuses on getting a better understanding of customer demands while centering on which existing companies haven't responded. Clayton Christensen's book *Competing Against Luck* [40] explains it as a theory that ascertains consumer choice when buying something. He describes that the first lesson is to discover which job consumers are hiring your product to do.

Jobs-to-be-done will help to identify the market opportunities and frame the future value proposition. This is done through in-depth customer empathy that helps determine their unserved requirements. The focus is on exploring the consumer's choices when buying something, not just on the surface but going deeper to establish the social, functional, and emotional dimensions of their decisions.

VALUE CHAIN ANALYSIS

After identifying the job-to-be-done we want to deliver, we must find new ways to perform these activities and bring new value. The value chain analysis will help us to reach this goal.

A value chain is a set of activities a company undertakes to deliver its offerings to the customer [41]. These activities include design, production, marketing, distribution, and customer service. The function of this analysis is to empower you to deliver higher value to untapped customer segments. This analysis includes but is not limited to fewer steps, more efficiency and cost optimization, which allows disruptors to offer unconventional efficiency. Fulfilling these conditions will move you a step ahead towards disruption.

BUSINESS MODEL

Disruptive innovation requires a structure, a blueprint, to begin with. As Haim Mendelson, the Kleiner Perkins Caufield & Byers Professor of Electronic Business and Commerce and Management at the Stanford Graduate School of Business, said, "Would you launch a new offer without a blueprint?"

The business model describes the market and the economic engine that will enable a business to meet its profitability and growth objectives. How is the business going to create value and generate revenue? If there is not value creation, the company will be unable to perform and will fail.

TECHNOLOGY

When planning disruption, businesses need to understand that technology can only aid by being an enabler, but it is not the sole requisite. In other words, the use of technology alone cannot disrupt an industry. Instead, to disrupt, technology must create new and more value. Thus, you need to identify the technology that enables you to offer the new value proposition.

At this stage, by combining these four pillars of unsettled disruption, you will be able to have a better view not only of the disruption potential in your industry but also a strategic orientation and plan to deploy "disruptive innovation."

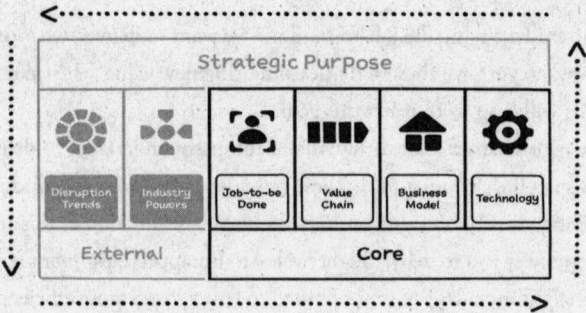

Figure 4- Unsettled Disruption - The Core Pillars

STRATEGIC PURPOSE

The COVID-19 pandemic has forced the world towards advancement. Businesses that heed it are progressing despite the imposed restrictions. In contrast, those who decided to stick to their traditional operations, paying no heed to the survival requisites, have met their fate: shut down.

Regardless of how devastating is the crisis we witness, it is also a wake-up call for a change, mostly an advancement. Now it's up to us to take this opportunity and improve, or ignore it and stay where we are.

Nowadays, consumers are much more inclined to support businesses that offer social and environmental benefits, driven by a strong purpose and putting sustainability at the core of their mission. A triggering factor pushing companies into adopting disruptive innovation can be the purpose that gives meaning to their existence. The "why" helps line up decisions. It also encourages businesses to test novel technologies, business models and innovation, and find ways to use them for good by fulfilling their purpose. The strategic purpose aims to set this ambition to establish the "why."

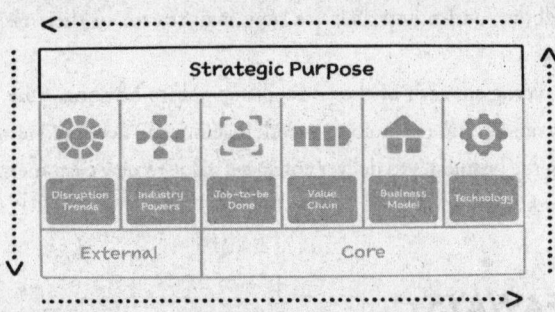

Figure 5 - Unsettled Disruption - Strategic Purpose

HOW THE UNSETTLED DISRUPTION FRAMEWORK WORKS TOGETHER

Since disruption is a dynamic process, the three levels of the unsettled disruption framework function and evolve together. A company's value chain, services, business model, and technology develop better value offerings for new customer segments over time. They will be all affected by external trends as we have experienced during the past years while playing around the different industry powers that change a company's situation.

For example, a new company, "X," offers new affordable goods to a niche market segment that cannot afford to buy the incumbent's offer. The formed incumbents are busy meeting their existing customers' demands which offers them a substantial profit margin despite their cost. When this new company comes into operation, it starts to evolve. As a result, its technology and value chain mature. They also begin testing different business models and learn. Soon, the new company can offer better products at an affordable rate than the incumbents can. With time, this enables them to serve the incumbents' segment of the market, along with its core segment. The moment the new company successfully targets the incumbents' customers and takes on mainstream customers and value, that's disruption. That is what happens with offers like Airbnb, Netflix, Slack, Zoom, and others that are now mainstream in their respective industries.

For doing so, each of the core pillars—job-to-be-done, value chain, business model, and technology—work together and develop one another, enabling the businesses to deliver enhanced value to new customers. That's what marks disruption.

TAKEAWAYS

The idea of unsettling disruption is followed by a ton of questions such as "Where to start? What to do? How to do it?" The best strategy to answer these questions is, to begin with, a systematic process that enables you to understand the internal and external elements influencing the market evolution to frame new opportunities.

Unsettled Disruption gives you the step-by-step guide to thoroughly understand the concept of disruption and put in place a plan to define your strategy. The primary three levels—external factors (trends and industry powers), the core pillars (job-to-be-done, value chain, business model, and technology), and the strategic purpose (why)—give you the structuring bricks that will be explained in the following chapters.

Disruption does not happen overnight, but all of these elements mature with time and eventually become powerful enough to disrupt an industry.

CHAPTER 4
DISRUPTION TRENDS

"Creativity isn't conceived as aiming at novelty or originality, but rather an integration."
Zhuangzi (莊子)

EIGHT YEARS AGO, I was discussing the strategy with an executive of a large beauty retail company. Both of us looked into the future of the industry. We talked about the opportunities for using mobile to diversify his company's channels. He knew that eCommerce had advanced quickly and attracted more customers than ever.

However, he believed that the beauty retail industry business attracts enough customers to the store. It's because they want to touch, feel, and try the products before buying. An essential part of the customer experience is to get personalized advice from the beauty expert at the retail store. That's the reason why his company was not interested in investing in mobile at that time. He further revealed that the company wanted to focus all its energy on attracting a physical footprint to optimize their investment.

Anyway, I asked him if he saw remote and mobile new trends as disruptive forces, and he shook his head to say "no." He was convinced that people love to come to the store and that this wouldn't change any time soon. He based his analysis on familiar and traditional factors such as diversification brought more money, international expansion is the goal, and the company's major competitor has opened new stores quickly, so we do. He was more comfortable with what he already knew.

However, I recently learned that there was a shakeup in this retail organization. The company decided to develop its digital strategy and stumbled upon mobile to exceed the customer experience remotely and in-store. During COVID-19 times, and thanks to this strategic shift, sales increased by 30 percent. This growth comes from their digital channel only, which compensated for the fact that they had to close some stores.

HOW KODAK FAILED

We cannot speak about disruption without mentioning Kodak; the company blew the opportunity of going digital in the early days [42]. How? Their R&D department developed the prototype of the first digital camera in the world. They presented the idea to the top management, who shot the whole thing down. They thought they would kill their best seller if they produced an alternative product. Management was so focused on selling original products and not evolving that they missed out on the most significant opportunities. Kodak could have become the digital camera industry's pioneer, but they didn't see it coming. They lost track of external trends and wanted to focus on their core business.

HOW WE MOVED FROM HARDWARE TO SOLUTIONS

It reminds me of my first experience in developing a corporate strategy. I started by doing an in-depth analysis of our direct competitors. I worked with different stakeholders for several months, and consolidated a three-year strategic plan with the support of several business units and regions. I also got the financial projections and R&D updates. I felt very proud as it was all based on the hardware business story, which, for more than fifteen years, was the core of the company's success.

At that time, my boss was visionary enough to understand the trend towards solutions-based businesses. So, he asked me to restart the process by analyzing the external disruption trends and our competitive industry position by looking into emerging players. Then he suggested that I needed to review our whole three-year plan from scratch. That was the beginning of our move from hardware to solutions for the next ten years.

WHY DECISION MAKERS FAIL AT IDENTIFYING DISRUPTION TRENDS

Tracking several variables gives you a number or two. And based on the numbers, stakeholders decide to avoid the false sense of security. Unfortunately, it results in the narrow-framing of the future. What happens next is failure due to disruptive forces that you never saw coming.

The only solution to the problem is to bring about change outside those known variables. We tend to not go out of our comfort zones because of odd threats. But we must consider unfamiliar areas of potential disruption and convert them into viable opportunities.

CHANGE IS DISRUPTING THE CURRENT SYSTEM

We heard that several experts predicted the pandemic, yet no one planned a proactive strategy. Countless retailers were not ready for digital transformation. But with COVID-19, they were forced to provide a touch-free shopping experience within just a few weeks.

Many companies get affected by such threats. Because the top executives don't see the change coming, they have a system that monitors and measures the known risks. Analyzing new disruptive forces in advance is rare in most companies.

The truth is that few companies saw a pandemic as a serious threat before the COVID-19. And honestly, we have several enormous challenges such as environment, climate change, and inequality throughout the planet's history right now that we are still ignoring. So, going beyond the known risks should be part of your strategy. Is your company ready for climate change or geopolitical revolution? Are you ready for more than 50 percent reduction in tourists and travels? Are you ready with an action plan for the disruption sources in your sector?

THE DISRUPTION TRENDS

The first step of unsettled disruption is to look into the environment and systems to identify different external disruption trends. This phase is inspired by one of the most important tools of business analysis that relies entirely on external factors: the "PESTLE" analysis [43]; and the work done by Amy Webb [44], a renowned futurist, described in her *MIT Sloan Review* article [45] "The 11 sources of Disruption every company must monitor."

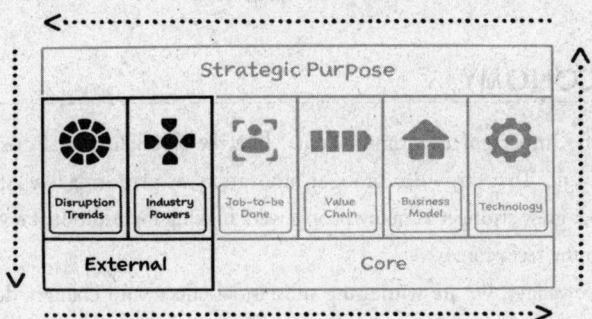

Figure 6 - Unsettled Disruption – External Factors

The disruption trends mapping will help you identify the potential areas of change in the future, and getting prepared for the colossal challenges brings a gigantic outcome. There is an extensive list of disruption factors to look for and learn to prepare for what could be the future. Ignoring them will leave even the biggest organizations vulnerable to disruption.

Let's have a look at each of them:

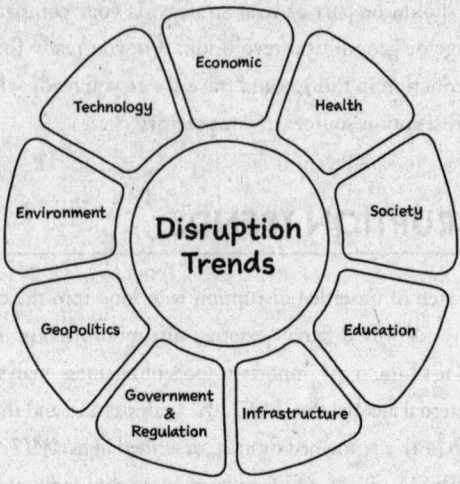

Figure 7 - Disruption Trends

1. ECONOMY

The impact of economic events, like the 2008 financial crisis, is significant. That crisis also brought innovation, as platforms like Airbnb or Uber grew stronger as many people were looking for additional revenue due to the recession.

Nowadays, we are witnessing substantial effects and changes during the COVID-19 pandemic. The first and foremost effect that we saw was the increase and decrease of certain items on the market. For example, toilet paper, masks, and sanitizer demand skyrocketed in the very first few days. Similarly, while some categories are experiencing a drastic increase in demand, others are slumping in the pandemic economy, such as luggage and cameras.

You need to look at the shift in standard macro- and micro-economic factors in the short and long term. But they only emerge if you are ready to take the plunge and get off the ground. Otherwise, you must have seen many businesses going bankrupt in response to the pandemic and other industries that were heavily affected.

2. HEALTH

Changes in the public health sector involve a lot of speculation in lifestyle, culture, and government regulation. The diseases, pandemics, warfare, and conflicts cause much tension in public health. Everyone has witnessed the adverse effect of the recent pandemic and how public health measures are changing several industries' entertainment, education, and tourism rules, just to mention a few.

3. SOCIETY

These factors scrutinize the social environment of the market, and gauge determinants like cultural trends, demographics, population analytics, etc. [46].

An example of this is the non-uniform distribution of wealth which causes much unrest in the world. We need to analyze the income of a population. The size of assets in communities also matters. Monitor the ability of people to climb from their current financial position.

The gap between the top and bottom segments within an economy plays an essential role in creating disruption forces. We have seen a radical change in these factors in developing and emerging countries, shifting consumption patterns.

For example, based on Pew's income band classification, China's middle class has been among the fastest-growing globally, swelling from 39.1 million people (3.1 percent of the population) in 2000 to roughly 707 million (50.8 percent of the population) in 2018 [47]. This significantly affects world consumption and sustainability patterns.

Another cause of disruption is the demographics of various kinds, including death rates, population density, and migration. When demographics change, everything changes from businesses to policies. This is today a significant source of disruption for several sectors in Europe. For countries where populations are aging, we will expect an increase in public spending on pensions, health care and others, along with emerging opportunities to develop new services.

4. EDUCATION

To identify the powerful disruption signal, we need to monitor people's access to education and training. We must closely examine what people are most interested in learning and what tools they are using.

After a couple of weeks of pandemic, the EdTech sector realized that learning institutions might not open for a considerable time. Therefore, it took a natural rise as most adopted the online route. Large-scale efforts to utilize technology in support of remote learning were made and they evolved at a fast pace. The EdTech sector has leapt to a prominent position, making it of particular interest to investors as it reshapes how we learn in real-time.

The World Bank believes we are in the grip of a learning crisis, where 60 percent of children globally fail to achieve minimum standards of reading and arithmetic because of poor quality teaching [48]. Even when students are learning, their education often doesn't include the skills they need to succeed at a time of unprecedented automation and technological disruption.

Today, the coronavirus pandemic has boosted the impact of EdTech like never before. I am looking forward to these new, better, and more efficient learning methods and to see how the traditional education system is being disrupted.

5. INFRASTRUCTURE

The physical and organizational infrastructure plays a crucial role in creating disruption forces. Such forces bring more bridges, power grids, WiFi towers, and security cameras. Currently, the cities are getting smarter with next-generation transport and communication. It affects businesses massively.

For example, we can recall the evolution of Mobile Phone Technology across the continent and how it opened the opportunity to create new businesses and tackle social issues in banking, health and education.

The ways we communicate and transfer information about the world on TV, social networks, and video platforms are gigantic sources of disruption. From gaming to e-sports and from social wars to getting 5G, every change allows more businesses to evolve.

6. GOVERNMENTS AND REGULATION

Businesses are heavily affected by local, national, and international governmental bodies. It would be best to keep an eye on how the government changes its policies. The planning cycle, election, and regulatory decisions create substantial disruption forces in the business community. We witnessed the government's abrupt change in response to the recent pandemic and how these decisions affected each country differently, including organizations, schools, and businesses.

These factors have both external and internal sides. There are certain laws that affect the business environment in a particular country while other policies maintain themselves regardless. The regulation considers both of these angles and then charts out the strategies in light of these legislations. For example, multiple businesses are being affected and forced into innovation because climate change policies affect industries such as mobility, packaging, food and others sectors.

7. GEOPOLITICS

Geopolitics also changes the scenario in our business community. The relationships between various leaders and militaries involve a lot of risks to companies across the globe. Just think about the global impact of Brexit and China-Russia relations.

These factors determine the extent to which a government may influence the economy or a certain industry. For example, a government may impose a new tax or duty due to which entire revenue-generating structures might change. Government automation is also changing the citizen's empowerment and access to services.

8. ENVIRONMENT

These factors include all those that influence or are determined by the surrounding environment. This aspect is crucial for most industries today, and includes factors such as weather, geographical location, global changes in climate and environmental offsets.

Abrupt climate change, rising sea levels, and temperature fluctuations have colossal effects on business disruption. Many industries are working on new services or offers and new ways to deliver better sustainability and reduction of their environmental impact.

Nowadays, the environment-related changes are massive compared to others. We are also seeing how consumers are becoming less tolerant of how companies operate against their interests. Environmental impact is changing the way we do business and redefining innovation.

9. TECHNOLOGY

Mobile, AI, virtual reality, Blockchain, 3D printing, and other technologies have changed the way people look at some businesses. We need to analyze the trend of emerging tech and other signals as enablers of change. We have seen high-speed disruption during the past year, thanks to the technology used to deliver their promise. Mobile phones and internet connectivity are making possible the evolution of services like Netflix, Airbnb and Uber.

Technology is changing the world and enabling new ways of doing business. A change in tech brings about more changes in how companies operate and reframe their value chain. We need to track technology innovation and define how that may affect the industry's operations and the market, favorably or unfavorably.

TAKEAWAYS

We have heard that several experts forecast the pandemic, yet no one planned a proactive strategy. Predicting the future is a serious task, but the experience tells us that we need to monitor what is happening outside our comfort zone.

The first level of the framework, "External," enables you to analyze disruption trends to connect the dots and understand better how such trends may impact your business. Many companies are affected because the top executives don't see the change coming. They have been surrounded by a system that monitors and measures only the known risks.

Analyzing the different disruption trends in advance will give you a competitive advantage to thrive in the world of disruption. You need to check which of these trends—economic, health, society, education, government regulations, geopolitics, environment, and technology—are more relevant to your business.

Remember, creativity is about connecting the dots. We must use all available information to understand the system better and get inspired by fresh opportunities.

Now we are ready for the next step of the unsettled disruption framework: to identify the threats and opportunities that make a business or industry prone to disruptive innovation.

CHAPTER 5
HOW TO ASSESS YOUR INDUSTRY

"If you're trying to disrupt the status quo and beat bigger competitors, you're not going to do it by playing their game."
Dharmesh Shah, OnStartups.com

SIXTEEN YEARS AGO, THE world was very different. In 2005, sending videos or big files through the web was a nightmare, an almost impossible mission. We carried with us our USB keys and even hard drives. Our relationship to music was awkward. We had a collection of CDs, and the idea of a streaming service for all the music we wanted was quite a shocking proposition. Not to mention our mobile phones—some of us had the privilege of getting media or emails via a boring user interface. We carried a maximum of three or four books in our luggage when we travelled, and finding our old high school friends' phone numbers was a wild goose chase.

Nowadays, we don't need to carry a USB drive; we have a drive on the Cloud with around one terabyte of storage space so we can have access to all kinds of pictures, videos, and files. We can carry thousands of songs on a digital music player or, even better, stream any track from anywhere via our sophisticated and connected mobile phones. We use our mobile phones to get our emails, handle our agendas, take pictures, in addition to networking, web browsing, and sometimes even calling our friends or messaging them via a WhatsApp group or the high school Facebook community.

At the moment, more sectors are constantly becoming the target of disruptors, banking, health care, real estate, air travel, and education, to mention a few. As stated in the *MIT Sloan Management Review* article, "Three Signals Your Industry Is About to Be Disrupted" [49], legacy companies are falling like dominoes to disruptors. Together, emerging technology and new business models have created different ways of serving customers. In the same way WhatsApp, iTunes, and Spotify have fundamentally changed the communication and music industries, titans such as Amazon, Google, and Facebook are now poised to disrupt every industry as wide-ranging as health insurers to grocers.

It's safe to say that no industry will be left untouched—but is yours next?

The previous chapter looked into the external sources that would help you map and understand the potential disruption trends. Now, you will look into assessing the factors that make your industry more prone to disruptive innovation by using Porter's Five Forces framework [41].

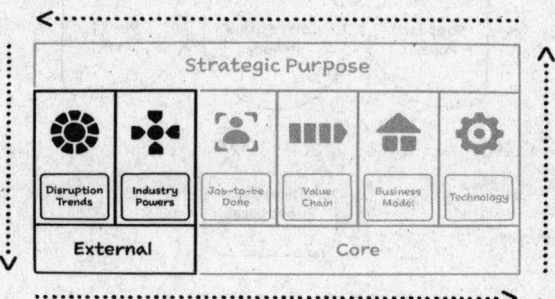

Figure 8 - Unsettled Disruption – External Factors

WHAT IS PORTER'S FIVE FORCES FRAMEWORK?

Porter's Five Forces by Michel Porter [50] is a tool for analyzing business and finding its profit potential. It helps to examine how attractive the sector would be for disruptors by scanning five forces, including:

- Buyer power
- Supplier power
- Threats of substitutes
- Competitive rivalry
- Threats of new entrants.

This framework helps us as a guideline to assess our industry and find out the possible opportunities and threats. Let's study each of these forces in detail. To illustrate how to use this analysis, we will use as an example the plastic packaging industry.

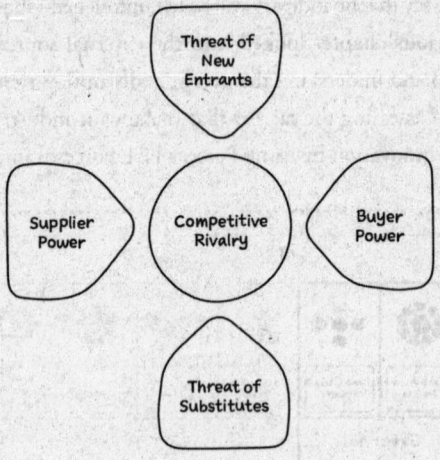

Figure 9 - Michael Porter's Five Forces

1. BUYER POWER

Buyer power is the extent to which your buyers can bargain on your product or service. To identify this aspect, you need to find answers to several questions.

How many buyers do you have? If you are offering a niche product or service, it means you have limited buyers. When you have few buyers, they are more powerful than you are. On the contrary, having more buyers gives you more power.

How many competitors are selling to your buyers? If there are few customers, but several producers of similar goods and services, then your customers have more options to explore. It increases their bargaining power and reduces your power.

Are there similar products available in the market? If there is a close substitute for your products in the market, then a slight variation can attract them towards or away from you.

Can your customers produce what you have to offer? When customers find sustainable and convenient ways to produce the goods and services you have to offer, they might stop paying you for them.

How easy is it for buyers to switch sellers? Switching sellers often costs buyers a hefty sum. If that's the case with your industry, you have the upper hand. However, if it's easy to change sellers, the buyers have many options among sellers.

HOW DOES BUYER POWER AFFECT DISRUPTION?

The profit potential of an industry is low when the buyers are more powerful. They have more control over the sellers' activities and decisions. Such an industry does not attract new entrants, hence reducing the chances of disruption; however, if the profit potential is high, the buyer power is low, making the industry more prone to disruption as it is attractive to new players.

ILLUSTRATION OF BUYER POWER IN THE PLASTIC PACKAGING INDUSTRY

Within the plastic packaging industry, buyers are big companies like Coca-Cola, Unilever, and PepsiCo, to mention a few.

1. Consumer goods brands, being super-competitive, demand high-quality products at lower costs.
2. These companies purchase bulk amounts in continuous cycles, which gives them better bargaining power.
3. Plastic packaging producers are constantly under pressure to produce customized and innovative goods to stand out from competitors and meet the buyers' individual needs. Therefore, they have to keep investing in innovation and differentiation.
4. The industry has challenging regulations and quality demands, which are difficult for suppliers to meet. Moreover, the sellers need to acquire a certificate to get into the business. This certification process increases the switching cost for buyers, which acts in favor of suppliers.
5. There is a low chance of backward integration threats from the buyers.

From these points, we can conclude that buyers' power in the plastic packaging industry is high, making the sector less attractive to disruptors. However, let's also keep in mind that the profit potential is high, due to the incredible volumes it represents.

2. SUPPLIER POWER

Suppliers are the companies that provide the goods and services used by other manufacturers to produce final goods. Thus, they involve every business from the manufacturer to the distributors. To evaluate supplier power, you need answers to the following questions.

How many suppliers are in the market? Are there more suppliers capable of meeting buyers' demands? If several suppliers are providing similar products, the buyers have more options to choose from. Also, if more suppliers can meet buyers' specific requirements, the ball rolls over to the buyers' court, reducing supplier power. Hence, if there are fewer suppliers in the industry overall, then buyer power shoots up.

What is the cost of switching suppliers? If the cost of switching suppliers is high, the buyers intend to stick to the same suppliers. This increases supplier power, to some extent.

How easy is it for suppliers to increase the prices? When there are fewer suppliers in the industry with high demand for their products, they develop better control over prices. They can charge the buyers a large sum for their products and services, affecting how they further produce and serve their customers.

HOW DOES SUPPLIER POWER AFFECT DISRUPTION?

Industries with higher supplier power are likely to face disruption because of greater profit potential. Disruptive innovation in such sectors requires vertical integration among suppliers, or the entry of new suppliers.

ILLUSTRATION OF SUPPLIER POWER IN THE PLASTIC PACKAGING INDUSTRY

Supplier power in the plastic packaging industry is low. Here's why.

- Several plastic manufacturers are offering a variety of raw materials for different buyers. Moreover, there are dominant suppliers with more innovative products, creating tough competition for others.
- The price-sensitive market and availability of substitutes limit suppliers' bargaining power. Hence, their control over prices is relatively minimal.
- The presence of a large number of suppliers reduces the switching cost for the buyers.
- Since suppliers provide materials to several segments, the chances of forward integration into the packaging industry are low.

3. THREAT OF SUBSTITUTION

Substitutes are the goods and services that can be used as an alternative to your offering. Suppliers in the industry producing similar goods as yours can devalue your product by a small variation in their products or prices.

For instance, if you offer a unique solution for transporting important goods, your buyers might find a way to deliver these goods by themselves. In this way, they'll provide a substitute for your product, threatening your profitability and shaking your position in the market.

HOW DOES THE THREAT OF SUBSTITUTION AFFECT DISRUPTION?

When there are already several substitutes available in the market, disruptors usually emerge from other related industries. They bring unconventional substitutes, giving the buyers something new to try and invest in. Therefore, to assess the risk of disruption in your industry in terms of substitutes, you need to think outside your industry's existing landscape.

ILLUSTRATION OF THE THREAT OF SUBSTITUTES IN THE PLASTIC PACKAGING INDUSTRY

The plastic packaging industry faces greater threat of substitutes. Due to increasing environmental awareness and regulations, people are switching to recyclable or biodegradable options, and new business models are emerging such as reuse, refill, and others. Consequently, manufacturers are coming up with better glass and metal products as an alternative to plastic. Yet they require more technological investment and substantial variations in the value chain.

The following are a few more reasons for the higher threat of substitutes in the plastic industry.

- Rising demand and significant revenue increase the threat of substitutes in the packaging industry. Companies with advanced technologies that can offer more cost-competitive options can easily pocket large profits.
- Eco-friendly packaging is the "new normal," and manufacturers have to follow new regulations and consumers' demands and trends.
- Environmental concerns and new regulations have imposed extreme challenges to the packaging market. It has ultimately affected the demand for packaging products by the consumer goods manufacturers because they are trying to protect both their revenue and image.

4. COMPETITIVE RIVALRY

Competitive rivalry refers to the amount of competition among the existing companies in the market. Industries with greater competition can force businesses to offer extreme price cuts and profit reduction. This requires businesses to invest more in marketing to achieve higher revenue than competitors. In such markets, it is easy for the buyers to switch suppliers if they are not satisfied with the provided goods or services. To find out the level of competition in your industry, you need to consider the following questions.

How many other companies are operating at a size equal to yours? If other companies are operating on the same scale as you, it means you have more significant competition. Therefore, it will require extra effort and inputs to make a better profit.

How loyal are the customers to their brands? Loyal customers tend to stick to their brands, making it difficult for other businesses, especially newer ones, to gain their target audience or revenue.

How fiercely do businesses in your industry compete? Businesses often offer extreme price-cuts or deals to customers to defeat their rivals. They bring about innovative ways to attract more customers, as investing more in marketing. Such situations often result in a substantial cut-down on their competitors' profits.

HOW DOES COMPETITIVE RIVALRY AFFECT DISRUPTION?

Industries with a high level of competitive rivalry are less attractive to new businesses as they are not as profitable. However, low competitive rivalry enables new entrants to make a better profit by offering something that others don't.

ILLUSTRATION OF COMPETITIVE RIVALRY IN THE PLASTIC PACKING INDUSTRY

Competitive rivalry in the plastic packaging industry is high.

- The industry has several big competitors like Reynolds Group and AMCOR, with revenues of over $10 billion [51]. Since several other suppliers have similar products, the competition is intense, as they compete to gain better market share, thereby reducing profit margins.
- Most suppliers are dedicated to fulfilling buyers' requirements, which limits the chances of product differentiation.

5. THREAT OF NEW ENTRANTS

The threat of new entrants means how easy it is for new suppliers to enter the market. Since each new entrant affects your position, you need to be careful about them. In a profitable industry with fewer entry barriers, the chances of new entrants are high. To find out how easily a new business can enter your industry, look at the following questions.

What is the upfront capital required to set up a business in your industry? Industries that require more significant initial capital to set up the business have lower chances of getting new entrants. Similarly, achieving economies of scale also restricts people from investing in certain companies.

What are the regulations to enter your market? Investors tend to avoid tightly regulated industries as they are difficult to penetrate or innovate. Moreover, industries dominated by some big names usually face lower threat of new entrants.

HOW DOES THE THREAT OF NEW ENTRANTS AFFECT DISRUPTION?

New entrants bring about new capacities and targets. They aim to gain a better market share, jeopardizing the position of existing businesses in the industry. If the barrier to entry is high, the chance of new entrants is reduced, and vice versa. Some examples of such barriers are government policies, large capital investments, greater customer loyalty for traditional brands, along with others.

ILLUSTRATION OF THE THREAT OF A NEW ENTRANT IN THE PLASTIC PACKAGING INDUSTRY

The threat of new entrants is relatively low in the plastic packaging industry.

- Several major producers are dominating the industry, which makes it difficult for new entrants to compete.
- The industry's capital investment is relatively high, discouraging investors from setting up a new business in the industry.
- More prominent and older companies producing large volumes can easily achieve economies of scale. However, for new entrants, it would be challenging.
- Extensive researches in the field and constant changes in designs are very expensive to bear.

- Government restrictions and certifications required by consumer goods manufacturers are other significant barriers to new entrants.

THE PLASTIC PACKAGING INDUSTRY IS PRONE TO DISRUPTION

The use of plastics has come under intense scrutiny in recent years. Prompted by headlines like "More plastic than fish in the oceans by 2050 [52]" and "UN commits to stop plastic ocean waste [53]," consumers and regulators have turned their attention to how to reduce plastic packaging consumption. These concerns regarding plastics are well past a tipping point of public concern and regulatory action.

So even if the entry barriers are high in the plastic packaging industry, balance in the remaining forces often offers sufficient profit to disruptors.

TAKEAWAYS

According to Porter's Forces, disruption is likely to occur in industries where the threat of new entrants and substitutes is more significant. In such situations, disruptors can find ways to overcome entry barriers and offer better substitutes. Even if the entry barriers are high, balance in remaining forces often offers sufficient profit to disruptors.

That's what we saw with the plastic packaging industry. Disrupters search for ways to shift power among the buyers and suppliers, leveraging environmental trends and regulations, then combining job-to-be-done opportunities with value chain, business model innovation, and technology.

Therefore, you can predict the chances of disruptive innovation in your industry using Porter's Five Forces [41] framework. According to it, if you are in a better position, move on to finding creative ways to innovate and offer better value to your customers. To assess your position, risks, and opportunities, study each of these forces thoroughly and write your observations. Note all the significant points and look into them to judge your situation and how they impact you from each of the five elements of the industry powers framework, that is, as buyers, suppliers, substitutes, new entrants and competitors.

Now that you have assessed your industry's risk of being disrupted, we just finished the external factors of the framework, disruption trends and industry powers. Let's start by gaining insight into the unsettled disruption core steps by understanding your customer's needs and defining the job-to-be-done.

CHAPTER 6
HONING IN ON JOBS-TO-BE-DONE

"People don't simply buy products or services; they hire them to make progress in specific circumstances."
Clayton Christensen

DURING THE PANDEMIC LOCKDOWN, we adopted a dog. The newcomer spent hours trying to catch the little lizards in the garden without any luck. I guess he could have wished for an easier or faster way to catch them, but he enjoyed the journey. I remember the last time we had a lizard in the house. I took some paper and Tupperware and caught the lizard to put it safely back in the garden. As we live in a rural area and this happens quite often, we created a system to catch lizards and free them easily.

The difference with my dog is that he can spend all his life hunting a lizard. Humans have an intrinsic desire to evolve themselves. We do this by remaking and adapting to the world around us. We use arts, sciences, and engineering to grow emotionally, intellectually, and socially. This need to evolve ourselves purposefully is what sets us apart from other animals. There was a time when humans grew tired of hunting down animals; therefore, they developed and moved to agriculture while domesticating animals. Unlike animals, for whom chasing the lizard can become a daily chore, humans will always look for more to do.

Jeff Bezos said, "Customers are always beautifully, wonderfully dissatisfied." That's the thing about humans. We are faced with a "job-to-be-done" every time we think of evolving ourselves.

JOBS TO BE DONE

According to Frost & Sullivan's research [54], one in 100 new products covers their development costs. McKinsey Global Innovation Survey [4] also shows that "although 84 percent of executives agree that innovation is important to growth strategy, only 6 percent are satisfied with its performance."

Innovation performance may be down, even if big data and AI technologies help to better understand the user. It is also a fact that human behavior is highly unpredictable. Hence, no data can ever provide a standard outlook of people's reactions, needs, and fears. Data may play an essential role in predicting buying and other patterns, but we can achieve better ways of ascertaining user needs. We must consider human behavior. We must define what job needs to be done.

This chapter is about one of the most exciting steps of unsettled disruption, defining "jobs-to-be-done." JTBD is the cornerstone of a better customer understanding and has a major impact on successful innovation. Christensen Institute [55] explains "Jobs-to-be-done as a theory that ascertains consumers' choices when buying something. These choices don't just scratch the surface but go beyond, thus determining the social, functional, and emotional dimensions of such decisions."

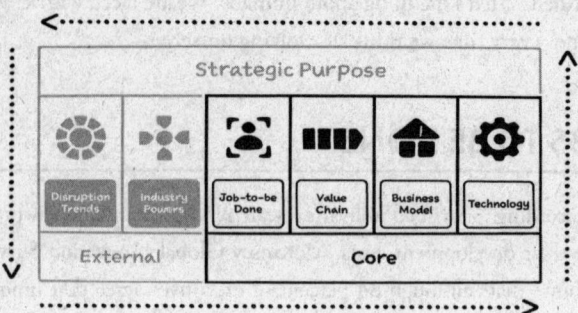

Figure 10 - Unsettled Disruption – Job-to-be-done

JTBD explains how people do not just buy stuff for the sake of it; instead, they buy for a specific purpose or, more precisely, to do a "job." By linking this necessity with progress, we home in on a world of innovative possibilities.

CAN SWEET POTATOES FOR DESSERT TRUMP CHOCOLATE PUDDING?

It happened twenty years ago; we were brainstorming with one of my best innovation partners, the R&D director of new product development. We wanted to find new ideas to reduce food waste and develop our frozen food portfolio. We had launched a successful product line of potatoes in the form of happy faces for kids. They loved it.

We thought at some point that we needed to expand this portfolio with other new ideas. We had some data that clearly showed that kids love potatoes in the form of French fries, mashed potatoes, and our new "happy faces." Therefore, we came up with a hypothesis that if kids love potatoes and sugar, they would love "sweet-flavored potatoes."

We did some tests and had some kids over for the first trials. Their first reaction was "Yuck!" My colleague looked disappointed as she had spent much time trying to find the best recipe, but I remember that she also smiled and said, "They hated it." That was the end of this adventure.

So, the data was there, potatoes were there, and sugar was there. However, there is no job-to-be-done by sweet potatoes. Potatoes are an excellent side dish for chicken or hamburger, but how do you dare to replace chocolate pudding with potatoes with sugar?

I know it sounds odd, but it was for real. At least we tried everything.

THE BUSINESS OF NOSTALGIA-FILLED HOPE

About two decades ago, we were looking for ideas to develop an offer for the US's Hispanic market, much in the same vein as we did with the sweet potatoes, but we onboarded the topic differently. We started by empathizing with our users.

After talking to Hispanic families residing in the US, we found that their key challenge was finding their traditional food in a foreign country. They missed home, and what they missed the most was things like "the homemade *arepa* that my mother did in the morning for breakfast," "I would love to have some *papas criollas*, but I can't find these here," or "in my country, we cook yucca sticks with fish. Here, I can't find a good yucca."

We realized that the job-to-be-done was not to provide the best French fries or best frozen food for this community. The job-to-be-done was to create a link between their community, their culture and roots, and delicious yucca chips—the moment of the nostalgia of having this special dish that they had in their countries.

So, we decided to develop a product line for Hispanics that brought the flavors of their country and culture. We started with yucca sticks and then expanded to other products. That was a hit; people were happy to find their roots in any supermarket in the US.

It was a tough deal to find local Hispanic food two decades back, while today, it's available everywhere.

INNOVATING BY MEETING JOBS-TO-BE-DONE

An in-depth understanding of jobs-to-be-done gives you the opportunity for innovation without any hint of your customers' trade-offs. If we check Nielsen BASES Breakthrough Innovation List for 2019 [56], the list of hits might seem random on the surface, but there are certain caveats. Every performer on the list catered a "job-to-be-done." Let's explore the JTBD with some examples, starting with "Kinder Surprise."

How did Kinder Surprise achieve breakout success with what might seem to be just another version of the decades-old peanut butter cup? Jobs aren't just about function—they have robust social and emotional dimensions. The folks at Kinder Surprise created a unique parents-kids experience.

Kinder Surprise is a one-of-a-kind product among the most successful confectionery launches of the past ten years. The product comes with chocolate and cream in one section and a little toy in the other. It is not just chocolate candy. The candy promotes healthy playtime between kids and parents.

THE HISTORY

Exchanging eggs to welcome the season of spring and fertility is an ancient custom. The Persians partook in it 5,000 years ago, and the Europeans took on the tradition in the late 1900s [57]. Originally, eggs were hand-painted with colorful dyes and then handed out to celebrate the tradition, but this changed in the early 1970s [58].

Michele Ferrero, the renowned Italian chocolatier, figured out how the egg-shaped molds could be used throughout the year instead of lying in the corner until Easter arrived. Thus began the new, unique, and lasting tradition of creating chocolate eggs [59].

It doesn't stop there: Ferrero wondered how the excitement that came with Easter could be preserved as well. This led to the creation of the Kinder Surprise—an egg-shaped mold carrying chocolate and toys. This product became extremely successful; it was launched in 1974, and until now, more than 30 billion Kinder Surprise eggs have been bought across the globe [60].

THE SURPRISE EGG JOB-TO-BE-DONE

The Kinder Surprise egg achieved success because Ferrero continuously improved his product using market insights and going beyond product features. He would leave unbranded prototypes of his product at a local supermarket in Luxembourg, which middle-class European families frequented. He would covertly hang around the market to listen and understand how shoppers responded to his product [61].

He soon realized that mothers were more likely to buy the Kinder Egg, but they had concerns about feeding their children too much sugar content with less nutritional value. As a result, Ferrero adjusted the recipe to include more milk, which worked because the mothers were more willing to give children sweets with more nutrition.

If we look at Kinder Surprise, the obvious customer segment is children. They cannot say "no" to chocolate, and they love toys. You combine the two into a single product and get something they cannot resist. But there is a more profound role for the surprise eggs.

If you go to a market, you will immediately see that the Kinder Surprise is placed right at the checkout counter. It gets noticed easily while you are waiting in line—by adults and children. Plus, the surprise factor of the egg works as a "variable reward." It's similar to the psychology that spurs on people in Vegas, sitting in front of slot machines, eagerly waiting to find out what they will get next.

When you get the egg and unwrap it excitedly, that's the part where your body will release the "pleasure chemical," i.e., dopamine. Studies have shown that dopamine, the pleasure chemical, reaches the brain not just when we get the reward but also when we are anticipating it.

Once the egg is unwrapped and the toy is revealed, then comes the part where parents work with children to assemble the toy. It's a sweet moment and encourages parent-child bonding.

However, it works with the Kinder Surprise because it triggers the cognitive bias, often known as the "IKEA Effect," where a person feels more attached to an item they create themselves. Using your energy to craft something allows you to feel a sense of ownership and accomplishment.

There are multiple facets of consumer psychology that this product targets. Therefore, it doesn't come as a surprise why it works. Let's remember that "job-to-be-done" isn't just about function—it has robust social and emotional dimensions.

ARE CUSTOMER EXPERIENCES SELLABLE COMMODITIES?

I remember my first visit to Starbucks. I was preparing for my GMAT and had a minimal budget because I was saving every cent for my MBA. How on earth was I willing to pay eight dollars for a vanilla latté and the corresponding carrot cake?

Because I spent four hours working in a lovely corner of the coffee shop, I loved it; it was a place in the downtown of the beautiful city I lived in at that time—Ketchum, Idaho. So, I didn't want a cup of coffee or even the best cup of coffee. I just wanted to enjoy these four hours' experience, working quietly to get the required score for my GMAT.

WHAT'S SO SPECIAL ABOUT STARBUCKS?

Starbucks' founder, Howard Schultz, said, "Starbucks has a role and a meaningful relationship with people that is not only about the coffee." Its mission: "To inspire and nurture the human spirit—one person, one cup, and one neighborhood at a time."

Starbucks was not always a home-like café that served cappuccinos and espressos; it was strictly a coffee and equipment seller in its early years. The café concept based on customer-centricity and user-experience emerged in the '90s when Howard Schultz [62] purchased the company and brought about its meteoric expansion.

Simon Sinek, the British-American author, described its success in this quote: "Starbucks was founded around the experience and the environment of its stores. Starbucks was about a space with comfortable chairs, lots of power outlets, tables, and desks at which we could work, and the option to spend as much time in their stores as we wanted without any pressure to buy. The coffee was incidental."

Starbucks' core principles include end-user understanding and customer experience. The company maintains the philosophy by encouraging brand loyalty through in-store services, where the staff is trained to cater to user needs and provide personalized services.

This customized form of service has made Starbucks a global player, with operations in over 80 markets and around 32,600 stores [62]. As of 2020, Starbucks-operated stores accounted for 81 percent of total revenue, while it yielded $23.5 billion revenue in 2020 [63].

PUTTING ON THE CUSTOMER HAT EARLY ON

The Starbucks founder, Howard Schultz, observed around 500 cafes in Milan and Verona [64]. Taking notes, videos, and photographs, he documented the baristas in action, studied the menus, the interior décor, and espresso-making techniques. After inspecting the inputs, he observed the customers—their habits, behaviors, likes, and dislikes, within particular "coffee" contexts. By developing his own taste palate for various coffees, he began to brew some for himself, roasted and took on the customer hat. Schultz's stepping into customer shoes was one of the main reasons behind Starbucks' phenomenal success.

In 2007, Schultz observed the user experience that had escalated Starbucks' growth [65]: It was fading. As the company evolved, he became aware of the pitfalls that continued to linger—the store no longer smelled of coffee beans, the customers began to complain about "cookie-cutter" layouts. To curb the weed before it grew, Schultz made a strategic move to close all 7,100 stores in February 2008 to school his staff with a three-hour training session. By taking a step back and slowing expansion, Schultz improved Starbucks' coffee-making by reintroducing smells, sights, and design elements that had once defined the brand.

The next president and CEO of Starbucks, Kevin Johnson, took over Starbucks in 2017 [66] and claimed that they were aware of its key issues and were determined to fix them. He further went on to say that their strength of customers, performance through morning and lunch day, new launches in food, beverage, and digital innovation were enough to make them confident in successfully fixing the problem.

The management at Starbucks then strived to singularize their stores across the world with regard to the sense of community, surroundings, and the coffee's taste and aroma that followed customers home on their sweaters. The stores differed in layouts, but the design elements remained the same.

Consequently, this approach was an instant hit—brand localization was one of Starbucks' creative efforts connected to its customers' job-to-be-done. Moreover, they strategically located design studios for the company to understand the customer community better. For instance, a Starbucks café in Times Square may feel theatrical inside, while the South may enjoy a weathered barn or blues music. Howard Schultz, former president, and CEO, describes the "Starbucks Experience" in his book *Onward* [67] as "our purpose and reason for being."

USING TECHNOLOGIES TO ENABLE THE JOB-TO-BE-DONE

According to Edgar Schein's *Organizational Culture and Leadership* [68], the processes may not be visible, but they are of the utmost value as defining the company's culture. Starbucks may not have a techy outlook, but technology is a big part of its strategy.

Starbucks' history is full of significant technological steps escalating its innovational strategies. In 1998, Starbucks was one of the first companies to have launched a website [69]. It began to provide free WiFi to its customers four years forward, which quickly transformed its brand from a regular coffee shop to an all-day hang-out place. Lastly, a decade ago, Starbucks established its social media presence on all platforms.

Moreover, while competitors of the company were still struggling to set up mobile payment channels and loyalty programs, Starbucks already had the model running. It has claimed to have received 24 percent of its orders and payments via smartphones in the fourth quarter of 2020 with 19.3 million active reward members [70].

Looking towards the future, the company is set to invest in millennials and Gen Z. It has launched gamified "Starbucks for Life" and Bingo promotions, which allow loyalty members to play games and earn points for free products [65]. Other examples of leveraging technology for expansion are the Starbucks Reorder Skill to Amazon Alexa platform in 2017 [70], which utilizes artificial intelligence. Similarly, the Starbucks Barista chatbot enables users to order their favorite beverages using voice commands.

WHAT IS SO UNUSUAL ABOUT STARBUCKS' CUSTOMER EXPERIENCE?

The reason why Starbucks is more popular than all other coffee brands across the globe is not that their coffees taste any better—although that might end up being a controversial statement for Starbucks fans—but because there's more to Starbucks than just the flavors.

Many coffee brands are producing better quality, better tasting, and even cheaper coffee than Starbucks. Some roadside shacks and retro cafés in Paris offer excellent coffee. Yet Starbucks' popularity remains unbeatable to date.

It is because, as an international tourist, you're more likely to visit a Starbucks in central Paris than go to a local coffee shop, unless you're up for some different experiences.

Users rarely like to see something different unless they don't have any other option. They visit Starbucks repeatedly because it is something that they are familiar with, and the other names of coffee shops sound alien. This relates the familiarity heuristics, defined as "judging events as more frequent or important because they are more familiar in memory."

HOMING IN ON JOBS-TO-BE-DONE

One of the striking aspects of "Great Brands" vision statements was that their statements were written or designed around their customers. This is reflected in Starbucks' Vision: "to inspire and nurture the human spirit—one person, one cup, and one neighborhood at a time." We can analyze this focus on end-users' job-to-be-done all around the Starbucks strategy as follows:

- **Solving problems:** A business's sole purpose is to solve a consumer's problem. Nobody is primarily interested in the product or service unless it can solve their problems. For example, some of Starbucks' problems are how to answer health-conscious customers' complaints about the unavailability of coffee options to brew at home.
- **Teaching customers:** Original Starbucks founders belonged to academia. Perhaps it was in their nature that their mission was not only to earn profits but to educate their customers about the joy of brewing top-class coffee and roasting the beans. They were passionate about hot beverages, refining the drinks' quality, and schooling their customers about the same. Following this thought, Starbucks leveraged the unique concept of baristas selling the beans and helping consumers make informed decisions about coffee beans, grinding, making, and brewing espressos. As a result, this customer-centric approach skyrocketed the brand's identity worldwide.
- **Sell the experience, not the product**: Starbucks is more about the experience than just the coffees. The baristas greet everyone cheerfully, and while making coffee, they make sure they strike up a conversation. Customers make small talk as the coffee brews, promoting a particular "Starbucks-exclusive" culture because, in

essence, the speakers are strangers to each other. The store is designed to enhance the quality of everything the customers see, touch, hear, smell, and taste. Particular attention is given to aroma, as it plays a vital role in the store's customer experience. The coffee-place meets the needs of various types of customers who visit the store at different times during the day. For instance, morning-time office-goers in a hurry are served on priority and as quickly as possible. In the afternoon, special care is given to mothers with children and retired folks who linger around to enjoy and relax. And similarly, in the evening, the store is the neighborhood's gathering place.

In essence, Starbucks coffee shops are designed to offer warmth and comfort to the customers' community as an extension of their homes. The management ensures each user experience is so memorable and joyful that first-timers come back again, and regular customers feel delighted every time they visit. Besides the usual ordering, paying, and leaving in a typical coffee shop, Starbucks offers these key pointers exclusive to the guest experience:

Always feeling welcomed: Sitting at a table from morning until evening is not uncommon at Starbucks. The brand is shaped to encourage customers who can barge in at any time and leave on their own, without ever feeling uninvited. This is one of the most cherished experiences shared by all Starbucks' customers alike.

Free WiFi: Who doesn't know about Starbucks for its free internet? Partnered with Google, the company facilitates its customer base with free internet to socialize, get the job done, or just hang out.

Blissful aroma: Starbucks' smell of coffee is unmatched. The coffee-makers make sure every store in every location has a signature tantalizing aroma exclusive to the brand's identity. By toying around with the sense of smell, Starbucks imprints itself in every memory.

Amazing offers for regular customers: Occasional Starbucks users might not relate to this, but Starbucks surprises their card-holders and regular users with some fantastic deals and offers from time to time. This can range from free coffee and discounts to loyalty rewards.

Starbucks has homed in on a job-to-be-done, to good effect. The company provides its users with a unique experience and charges a premium for it, thus running 32,600 stores in 2020 [62]. This customized form of servicing has made Starbucks a global player, with operations in over 80 markets: As of 2020, Starbucks-operated stores accounted for 81 percent of total revenue, while it yielded $23.5 billion revenue [63].

TAKEAWAYS

Every organization involved in a disruption process reaps different fruits because the methods differ considerably. Companies look at data to predict customer behaviors but ultimately fail due to the non-recognition of jobs-to-be-done.

By starting to onboard the core of your unsettled disruption journey, you need to focus first on empathizing with the customer and understanding the fundamental drivers to define which job-to-be-done is the ground for your disruption road. JTBD explains "how people do not just buy stuff for the sake of it; instead, they buy for a specific purpose or, more precisely, to do a job." [40] By linking this necessity with progress, we home in on a world of innovative possibilities.

Companies that identify these trends will undoubtedly cater to the needs of the customer in a different dimension. Jobs-to-be-done relates not just to the offer but to all elements related to the user experiences. Starbucks and Kinder Surprise excel at providing value to their customers by combining an offer or service, aligning value chain processes, developing a business model, using technology, and designing an exceptional user experience to stay ahead of the curve.

But it is not easy to identify these jobs-to-be-done. In the next chapter, we will discuss the challenges to establish real value for the customers when using the unsettled disruption framework.

CHAPTER 7
FIVE MOST COMMON JOBS-TO-BE-DONE CHALLENGES

"Once you understand what jobs people are striving to do, it becomes easier to predict what products or services they will take up and which will fall flat."
Stephen Wunker

THE AVERAGE TIME SPENT on the S&P by any business is a marker for that company's stability. This figure continues to shrink; in 1960, it was 33 years; in 2016, it was about 24 years; and it's forecast to be just 12 years by 2027 [71]. There are several reasons why organizations fall off this ladder of success, including being overtaken by a faster-growing company or a merger.

Another reason for this sharp demise from the coveted list is that it has never been easier to create new products. Supply chain optimization leads to a better reach of customers within months of their conception; this fast pace increases the speed at which innovations disrupt the established market and then replace the incumbents.

"Jobs-to-be-done" provides a way of understanding the foundational question of innovation success: what causes customers to purchase and use a particular product or service? In other words, the value of a product is not about the physical features only. Instead, it is what the product does for the end customer. Hence, it is to fulfill the newest need of the hour that innovators start producing products that help customers achieve their goals and objectives; in other words, make their lives better.

Jobs-to-be-done can be the hard-learned lessons that product managers, developers, marketers, and innovators need to adopt to enter a new paradigm about the real meaning of value-for-customers.

In this chapter, and inspired by Alan Klement's book, *When Coffee & Kale Compete* [72], you will go deep into some of the challenges to identify jobs-to-be-done. These challenges help to go beyond superficial categories to expose the functional, social, and emotional dimensions that explain why customers make the choices they do.

1. CREATIVE DESTRUCTION IS ON THE RISE

At some point, I was curious to test a "no-code" service platform named "Glide" that enables the user to create a mobile application using a Google sheet. Yes, it's that easy. I was very proud of my output, a rudimentary prototype that took me only two hours. After its completion, though, I started to wonder how many companies focusing on developing mobile apps will be disrupted by this new service. This process is known as "creative destruction," and it has been on the rise, thanks to technology.

Creative destruction isn't new; what is new is the speed of the change. In *The Origin of Species* [73], published in 1859, Charles Darwin wrote that the "extinction of old forms is the almost inevitable consequence of new forms' production." We know that the extinction of the dinosaurs facilitated the adaptive radiation of mammals. In this case, creation was the consequence rather than the cause of destruction. But this transformation took millions of years.

Now, change is taking place at a rapid pace. This is seen through a company's lifespan, expected to be reduced from 33 years in 1960 to 12 years by 2027 [71]. What has been common since time immemorial is that destruction begets a new spirit of creation. For example, the scarcity of wood and everyday life's needs forced humans to discover substitutes for wood. It also forced the use of coal for heating, coke invention to produce iron, and many more processes to meet a basic need.

When one innovation wins, another loses. Why? Because a day has only a few hours for a customer to spend on multiple products. For example, I used to get a café latté from a coffee shop on my way to work every morning. During the COVID-19 lockdown, I bought a coffee machine that makes a fabulous and fresh latté. Now I make my latté, and subsequently, the coffee shop has lost my business.

The global pandemic has accelerated this creative destruction; we see more and more new businesses arise while others struggle to survive. I mentor several entrepreneurs and startups looking to carve a way out of this disastrous situation. These companies are doing this by being creative and extremely reactive to external stimuli. They start their journey by getting deep into analyzing how customers' priorities changed.

2. WE DON'T TAKE INTO CONSIDERATION HOW CUSTOMERS SEE COMPETITION

Most of the time, companies see competition in terms of product category, such as the best digital camera or the most outstanding television. The "jobs-to-be-done" theory lets us look at competition from different perspectives. It isn't about the best in a specified class but how customers can benefit from such a product to make their lives better.

Kodak and the digital camera manufacturers never foresaw that a mobile phone could become their principal competitor. To succeed, you need to see how customers view competition. Does a television compete with television only? Or does it compete with the internet, outdoor activities, online games, and other recreational activities?

Going further, just think about Netflix, the leading streaming service provider that offers a wide variety of award-winning TV shows, movies, anime and documentaries that consider our need for sleep as one of its main competitors [74].

This new perspective will help you to better understand the customer view on what does and doesn't count as competition for a JTBD (job-to-be-done).

3. FOCUSING ON THE CUSTOMER'S PRESENT NEEDS, RATHER THAN CREATING NEW SYSTEMS FOR THE CUSTOMER TO PROGRESS

The 1860s introduced a company by the name of Pony Express. [75] It burst on the scene of mail services. It sprang up to facilitate customers sending their letters or messages across state lines and it used relays of horse-mounted riders. Although the company provided a speedy way to communicate, it only lasted about nineteen months. What was the reason behind this sharp decline, you may ask?

The answer is Western Union [76], a company that sought out an even quicker way of communicating. The telegraph became a revolutionary change in people's lives as it made the written or "physical" mail somewhat redundant. The transcontinental telegraph by Western Union looked to the future, whereas Pony Express was only looking to solve the common man's current need for physical mail. Western Union thought along the lines of "What if we can let customers communicate without the physical messages?"

Focusing only on the current customer's needs won't get you so far in terms of disruption. The real innovation lies in creating systems to help users progress in their daily lives.

Innovators are in the business of studying customers' needs, but what they forget often is that these insights can be misunderstood. Customers' needs can relate to the problems or complaints they may have of the current product, or show what the customers expect in a newer product. Hence, innovators get blindsided by assuming that these are actual needs; instead, they're just feedback on using a certain product.

An excellent example to demonstrate this erroneous data reading is shown by giants such as Nokia, Palm, Research in Motion (RIM), and

Motorola. These companies worked tirelessly to fulfill their customers' expectations. They thought that an affordable mobile phone with a physical keyboard was the need of the hour. Instead, we can see how users these days don't shy away from paying hundreds of dollars for a keyboard-less smartphone. The physical keyboard on a smartphone is redundant nowadays.

If companies think about it, and ask, "What if we give our customers a smartphone with no keyboard? Would it help them progress further?" then they may stand a chance of creating something unique.

These examples tell us that if we want to disrupt and create products for the future, we cannot look at today's products. Customers sometimes don't even know what they need until they get it. For this reason, innovators must look at one guiding principle to enhance innovation: customers and their quest for progress. The change and innovation that result from focusing on the customer's progress rather than their needs is futuristic. There are no limitations when you think this way. The current products' restrictions are lifted from their shoulders, and the canvas is blank to repaint from scratch.

To adopt a strategy that looks to the future, we should begin assuming that tomorrow may not resemble today. It involves looking into customers' jobs-to-be-done, dominant future trends, and the external sources of disruption described in Chapter 4.

4. THE INERTIAL COST OF LEGACY

When a Kodak [42] engineer in 1975 made a breakthrough by inventing the digital camera, Kodak's management response was anticlimactic. The management decided to shelve the digital camera, citing such reasons as their productivity would be smashed. They were alluding to the billion-dollar sales Kodak made selling photographic films. The photographic film would have thereby become redundant upon the advent of a digital camera.

It is quite common to see that it's legacy rather than technology that stops big organizations, or even small ones, from adapting and innovating.

Most recently, I was part of a company portfolio review. This was a yearly meeting where product managers had twenty minutes to share their offer status, project, and resource needs. Many of them were asking for more time to prove their offer value. Even though they had spent several years trying to achieve their objectives, or even when it was clear that their product was at the end of its life, the most repeated argument was, "We had spent millions on this product so we must continue! Why should we change when we can make a few more millions?"

The difficulty of leaving a "legacy" is not limited to the big corporations but also extends to entrepreneurs. While working with entrepreneurs, it is often the case that they argue to keep the current status of their products alive. They claim that they have spent a lot of time and effort working on their offer. These excuses may sound reasonable at times, but make innovations in businesses a bit harder. What companies forget is that if they don't adapt or change, someone else will do it.

5. DATA IS HELPFUL, BUT IN A HOLISTIC MANNER

The Net Promoter Score (NPS) is a popular system for analyzing customer experience based on surveys. For one of my former employers, we implemented NPS to ascertain customer experiences. In the beginning, we looked to customers to give feedback regarding their satisfaction with our services. To achieve this, we conducted face-to-face interviews.

As the company grew, we moved to a self-report model with online survey-based responses. If the NPS was higher than the previous year, it meant we were going on an upward trajectory. The numbers could let us make simple assumptions and offer some clarity. Simultaneously, though, they could also hide insights and opportunities that the interviews duly provided.

The new data and figures were incomplete at best and misinformation at their worst. So, we decided to go back to our tried and tested formula of interviewing customers. It helped us understand customers' challenges and future needs; meanwhile, we kept the online survey as a global indicator of sorts.

Ronald Coase, British economist, said, "If you torture the data long enough, they will tell you whatever you want." Figures can often be misleading or even misused. Just remember how we saw the explosive figures of Facebook, and began making assumptions. However, we also judge its business model; yet its market cap as of December 30, 2020, was $788.98 billion [77].

In the same vein, Twitter has grown exponentially. In the last five years, its revenue had risen from $106 million in 2011 to $3.46 billion annually in 2019 [78]. Despite these staggering numbers, analysts as well as journalists seem to write off Twitter and publish pieces such as "The End of Twitter [79]." Why, may you ask? The reason for this criticism comes from a deeper problem that looks at Twitter's growth in numbers a bit differently. Looking at the numbers, Twitter's MAU (monthly active users) may seem stuck at 330 million [80].

Thus, the management can see this as stagnation and feel the obligation to increase users' numbers, but the vital question for Twitter should be, why not focus on the existing customers? Chopping and changing too much may get you many new users, hence a better MAU (monthly active users), but it may drive other users away in the long run. As the grandmother's advice goes, "If you try to please everyone, you may end up pleasing nobody."

Many managers and innovators seem to be influenced by notions such as "measurement is the key to managing things." Data may be an essential part of analyzing something, but it may prove disastrous if used without any context of a system's knowns and unknowns. The most damaging result of just using data for a complete analysis is that the numbers can paint a false picture. The visible figures may point towards excellent sales, but they may hide a particular product's flaws, resulting in stagnation. This stagnation will almost inevitably result in overconfidence that the product will last forever.

If you're still trapped in yesterday's assumptions by using today's data for the sake of extrapolating future values, you may need to think again. Dynamic environments react to data differently, and hence this data usually puts constraints on choices and opportunities to expand the business.

TAKEAWAYS

Disruptive innovation can be risky, nerve-wracking, and indeed hard for managers and entrepreneurs. Even those who have been successful at this art will tell you that it is a daunting task. It is often seen that managers fail to grasp these challenges related to customer jobs-to-be-done. A predisposition related to slowing sales may blind us to discard innovative solutions and start with such short-term actions as lowering prices, offering newer features, and changing for change that may entice some new users, but it is detrimental to the company in the long run.

Jobs-to-be-done enables understanding of innovation's foundational question, which causes a customer to purchase or use a particular product or service. But on this road, there are challenges to recognize why customers make the choices they do. We need to consider the accelerated speed of creative destruction, looking beyond traditional competition, and empathize with the customer's perception of who we are competing with.

Other pitfalls include focusing only on the present instead of on the systems to enable customer progress, the inertial legacy of the cost that deters us from taking a new risk, and finally, being trapped in yesterday's assumptions by extrapolating data without looking into external factors and competitive landscape.

Now that you have a better view of the first phase of the core of unsettled disruption—job-to-be-done—you have probably started to uncover your sector's opportunities. The next chapter will start with the second step to determine how to deliver your disruptive value proposition to a customer by analyzing and framing your value chain.

CHAPTER 8
THE "HOW" BEHIND VALUE CHAIN DISRUPTION

"Our shared vision of belonging is the thread that weaves through every touchpoint on Airbnb."
Brian Chesky

I REMEMBER A ROAD trip as a beautiful experience, a moment to enjoy the landscape, visiting while stopping here and there. Still, it can also be an expensive option when using your car and driving alone, or even boring when you have to travel several times per month. Not always an adventure.

As we are looking for sustainable answers to our mobility needs and the industry is facing additional urgency to reduce carbon emissions, Mobility is one of the sectors where disruption trends and competitive pressure have increased. This has translated into new and successful business models and value chains presented by companies such as Uber, Lyft, Easy Mile, ZipCar, and BlaBlaCar.

Did you know that according to transportation adviser Paul Barter, the average car spends about 95 percent of its time parked? [81] For example, BlaBlaCar, a company that disrupts, created value by connecting riders' empty seats with passengers looking for an inexpensive trip. As of 2021, they have built a community of 90 million members, [82] providing last-minute travel options and cost savings for both drivers and passengers around trustworthy carpooling.

BlaBlaCar offers an inexpensive travel option for passengers compared to flights or trains, which are expensive, especially when booked at the last minute. Apart from savings, BlaBlaCar offers a great social experience (versus driving or traveling alone). They shook up traditional bus lines and trains more than taxis or other intra-city car-sharing services such as Uber and Lyft. BlaBlaCar has strengthened its position in the market as one of the most trustworthy carpooling services.

BlaBlaCar put all pieces together to provide that experience, and this creation of value for new customers is how disruption works. This "how" is the center of this chapter's attention through the second phase of the unsettled disruption core, the "value chain."

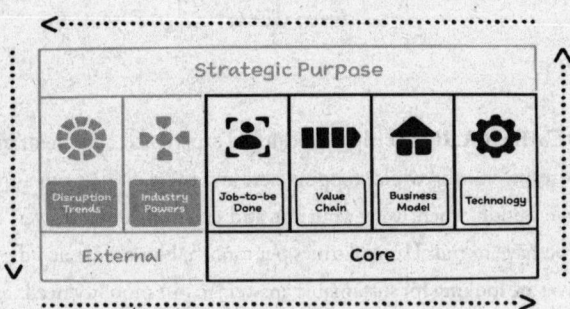

Figure 11- Unsettled Disruption – The Value Chain

HOW DOES VALUE CHAIN DISRUPTION OCCUR?

Michael Porter of the Harvard Business School came up with the term "value chain" in 1985 [83], describing a set of activities from initiation to delivering the product to the customer's doorstep. These included designing, production, marketing, logistics, and customer support. A value chain merely relates to the efficient ways of completing each step for delivering higher end-user value.

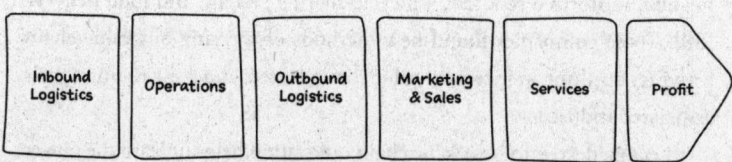

Figure 12 - Michael Porter's Value Chain

Creating a value chain with fewer steps or more efficient ones leads to customers getting more value from a product. The producer also benefits from better productivity or even cost reductions [84].

Twenty years ago, new entrants found a difficult entry into the industries sector. However, with information flows improving and customer expectations changing, this trend has changed. New entrants can reduce costs by eliminating low-value stages from the value chain, or relying on others to perform such processes, thus helping them gain value for themselves and their customers.

Thanks to technology and innovation, value chains are continually evolving. Their processes are streamlined and made more efficient, including larger value chains with complex operations that could be trimmed down.

Customers influence the value chain stages. In some cases, it results in lower prices, as IKEA describes by saying that "We can't do it alone. Our business idea is based on a partnership with the customer." [85] They cannot achieve value chain by streaming alone; the partnership with customers is essential for a more cost-effective product.

Disrupters look to shorten the value chain by removing intermediaries. These intermediaries complement the value chain, but by eliminating steps, new entrants save valuable costs. An example of this cost-cutting endeavor is when Warby Parker [86] eyewear market disruptor decided to stream their commercial process by selling their glasses directly to the customers.

One of the most prominent examples of streamlined value chains can be seen in new entrants to the digital marketplace. Companies as Kiva, a non-profit organization that allows people to lend money via the Internet to low-income entrepreneurs [87], or Lyft offering vehicles for hire, motorized scooters, a bicycle-sharing system, and food delivery [88]. These companies found new methods of carrying out value chain activities resulting in increased value for end-users and a shake-up in their associated industries.

Let's go deep into how value chain innovation helps unleash the power of disruption in each of the following industries.

DELL DISPLACES EXISTING PC POWERHOUSES

In 1985, Dell [89] disrupted the traditional PC market value chain by implementing a new distribution strategy and offering built-to-order computers. That year, the company generated $70 million in sales. Five years later, revenues climbed to $500 million, and by the end of 2000, Dell's revenues reached an astounding $25 billion [89].

Dell's fortunes changed when it adopted a business model that bypassed distributors and resellers, who were, at the time, a significant part of the PC value chain. This strategy led to a huge company that originated in a dormitory, outpacing giants such as Compaq, Packard Bell, and IBM by 2000 [90].

The direct sales model offered a customizable and accessible way for customers to get what they wanted. Customers had the option of selecting different components. This model also helped the company reduce costs, especially channel costs, which came down from 13.5 percent to just 2 percent of revenue [91]. Other former powerhouses, such as Compaq, failed to adapt effectively as their business models relied on distributors and retailers.

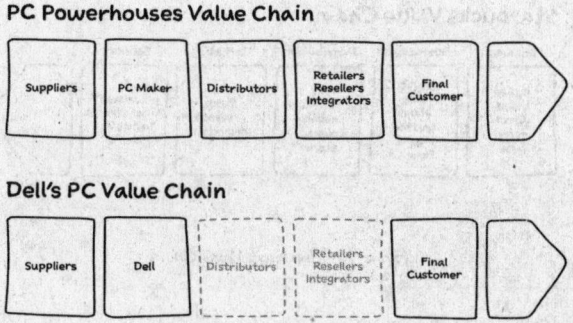

Figure 13 - Traditional PC vs. Dell Value Chain

A change in strategy meant uplifting the whole system and discontinuing the partnership that had offered a steady revenue stream. Dell's model also required creating a complex delivery system, infrastructure, and in-house capabilities that retailers had been providing.

Dell became the leader due to the most efficient path that helped them to better understand customers' needs via direct relations, customized offers, and superior and tailored services. In the third quarter of 2020, Dell held a 15.2 percent share of global PC unit shipments [92], while Compaq is no more on the map. Meanwhile, as market dynamics change, Lenovo and Hewlett Packard have emerged as the new market leaders.

STARBUCKS AND ITS VALUE CHAIN EXPERIENCE

Starbucks is an entity that offers some interest purely due to its value chain perspective, which provides considerable benefits to the customer. The company changed the landscape from supply to customer care and uprooted the traditional coffee shop model from procurement to distribution.

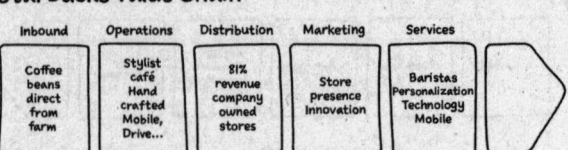

Figure 14 - Starbucks Value Chain

The logistics of coffee bean procurement sheds some light on the Starbucks value chain. Buyers across Africa, Latin America, and Asia appointed by the company buy fine quality beans and send them back to the mainland for storage and further processing. At the heart of Starbucks' strategy is that it doesn't outsource the beans' procurement, thus ensuring the highest quality. The proprietary packaging and roasting also help increase the value of the beans. The post-processed beans are then sent to distribution centers, some of which are owned by the company [93].

The focus of Starbucks' value chain is to ensure high-quality products and superior customer satisfaction. Marketing comes second and is done on a need basis. The marketing activities are carried out during product launches and sampling in new areas.

Customer experience is at the center of Starbucks' philosophy. It is maintained through harnessing loyalty for the brand through its in-store services. Value added is ensured by training the staff to cater to customer needs and offering personalization.

On the top, Starbucks is also a leader in integrating technology to support these smooth customer experiences. From ensuring strict quality control through technological innovations, to connecting customers and letting them work from the shop by providing WiFi, Starbucks has it all. It also offers in-app notification, thanks to Apple's iBeacon system so that the customer gets notified when their order is ready. With around 30,326 stores [94], Starbucks is a global player with operations in over 80 markets [95].

AIRBNB ACCOMMODATION WITH NO PHYSICAL ASSETS

Airbnb is an example of the underlying value chain mechanisms that make disruption possible.

First, they identified a job-to-be-done, i.e., people needed more affordable housing. Then there was the sense that customers would not mind staying in a stranger's house as long as they were assured that it would be safe. This need got more demanding once the 2008 financial crisis hit the global economy, and many people wanted to generate some extra money by hosting travelers.

As we have seen in this chapter, a value chain includes a set of activities that the business carries out to bring value to its customers. Airbnb's value chain insight was that their business did not need to own and maintain certain assets in order to deliver their value proposition. For Airbnb, these assets were rooms. Instead of owning rooms, Airbnb would enable other people who owned rooms to lease those assets to their customers.

Traditional Hotel Value Chain

Inbound	Operations	Distribution	Marketing	Services
Find a place Build a place Rent a place	Clean Prepare Receive Provide info Host	Travel agencies Aggregators Call center	Advertise Reservation Schedule Social	Insurance Additional Services Offers

Airbnb Value Chain

Inbound	Operations	Distribution	Marketing	Services
Find a place Build a place Rent a place	Clean Prepare Receive Provide info Host	Website App Network effect	Advertise Reservation Schedule	Insurance Additional Services Offers

Figure 15 - Traditional Hotel Chain vs. Airbnb Value Chain

Airbnb disrupted the traditional hospitality value chain. They don't own any physical properties and found a way to connect room owners with travelers. It accomplished this by relying on technology, while the hosts bore the operational costs.

The company could then facilitate the process of connecting travelers with homeowners through a digital marketplace. Thus, the insight, that physical rooms aren't needed to deliver value, is Airbnb's value chain model's crux.

According to Airbnb data, as of September 2020, there are more than 5.6 million listings, 4 million hosts, and the platform had expanded to more than 220 regions and countries [96].

IKEA FROM PASSIVE TO ACTIVE BUYERS

The first time I discovered IKEA was during my arrival in France, moving from the US. I realized that I needed to fill my new apartment quickly. That's where assembling my furniture came into play with some help, of course.

IKEA identified a job-to-be-done of making fashionable furniture accessible on a mass scale. For people with this need for furniture that could be easily transported and was affordable, IKEA's ready-to-assemble furniture became an instant hit. This new furniture model, sold as condensed and unassembled pieces, has allowed IKEA to reduce the raw material, shipping, and storage costs. It also eliminated expenses related to the order-taking and fulfillment stages.

The in-store experience also results in more customer engagement with increased efficiency due to removing the typical lag between a customer picking out the furniture and receiving it. IKEA customers have the comfort of buying and assembling on the same day.

IKEA offers clients more than just low prices—it has changed the model of how businesses interact with them by cultivating a shift in customer mindset. The change from passive buyers to becoming active participants mobilizes users to create product value. On the top, other products and services at IKEA stores such as paper pads, plenty of pencils, in-store restaurants, and childcare facilities make visitors feel at home.

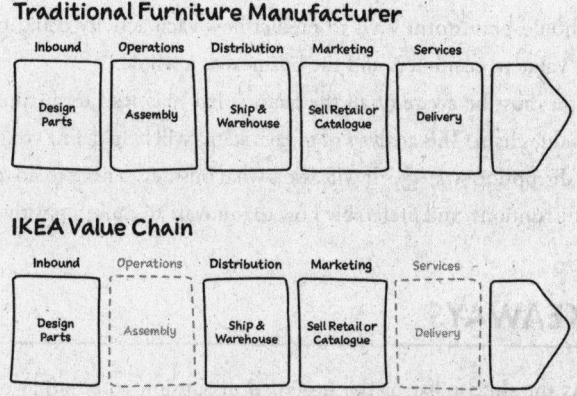

Figure 16- Traditional Furniture Manufacturer vs. IKEA Value Chain

The promise to keep prices low if users can assemble the furniture at home is a subtle promise that goes a long way towards boosting sales. All these factors helped build the brand IKEA into what it is today. IKEA not only shortened the value chain but "systematically reinvented its value and the business system that delivers it to the actors involved." [97]

IKEA became the world's largest furniture retailer with 445 stores worldwide [98] and 41.3 billion Euros global revenue in 2019 [99], due to unique value delivery and customer engagement. Most incumbent businesses may hesitate to transition to an IKEA-like model. They still fear pushing away customers who are unwilling to take on tasks traditionally defined as a supplier's responsibilities.

VALUE CHAIN ANALYSIS

A value chain analysis requires considerable research and time to develop. First, you need to determine the primary vs. support activities of a business. These are necessary activities for developing a product or service, from its raw material phase to the final product. Then you must analyze the value and cost of each activity and identify any room for improvement. You should brainstorm ways to predict how each activity could provide better value to customers and the business as a whole.

You must be aware of all the factors that may lead to disruption in your value chain. This analysis of today's status will help define your "value chain disruption strategy." It will assess what businesses need to do to avoid such disruptions, and preferably how to innovate to cause a positive cycle.

TAKEAWAYS

As the third pillar of the unsettled disruption core framework, the value chain analysis helps innovators look beyond standard means of efficiency and look for ideas to disrupt the status quo. This breakdown leads to an overall identification of how disruption occurs in a market or how to disrupt one's very own value chain.

As seen in this chapter, shortening the value chain has already disrupted the existing powerhouses in multiple industries, such as PC manufacturers, retail furniture, hospitality, and tech-related sectors. Other sectors that are realizing the full potential of technological advancements will be vulnerable in the future. These include industries with long or complex value chains and high costs relative to the value of technology-driven disruptions. An example is health care, where technology is already making inroads using telemedicine to gain immense popularity with customers and healthcare providers alike.

Across industries, advances in digital or manufacturing technologies and shifting customer mindsets may create opportunities to shorten the value chain. New entrants experimenting with technology may discover new options to remove parts of the value chain. Businesses these days are increasingly becoming volatile, with many factors affecting their productivity and maintenance. Value chain disruption will help streamline your processes by removing redundancies and increasing each step's efficiency.

In the previous chapters, you started your unsettled disruption journey by looking into external factors and learning how to assess the environment and your industry to identify potential disruptive trends and the risks of being disrupted. Then, you started to focus on the core of the framework by analyzing customer needs to find "job-to-be-done" opportunities. The second step is the value chain analysis as a fundamental brick of finding new ways to deliver the jobs-to-be-done value. The next chapter looks at building an innovative architectural framework to put the pieces together to make your disruption possible, the "business model innovation."

CHAPTER 9
BUSINESS MODEL INNOVATION

"The reason why it is so difficult for existing firms to capitalize on disruptive innovations is that their processes and their business model that make them good at the existing business actually make them bad at competing for the disruption."
Clayton M. Christensen

THAT EVENING OF 2007 in the autumn, I was digging into Chris Anderson's book *Free* [100], searching for inspiration to support a new business model proposal. We were launching a novel offer, and I was required to revamp our original model. So, I was going to present to the innovation board a "freemium model," which was a disruptive approach at that time for a very traditional company.

After almost twelve years, I faced the same challenge while suggesting that a customer move on from their initial one-set-up-fee model to a subscription model. It took me three months to convince him. I was lucky enough to have one of his biggest customers asking for it. So, in the end, he decided to give it a try. Even if he was afraid of losing his hefty setup fee business, we developed the subscription model for all his customers after a successful test. Today, his business gets better customer engagement and is ensured hefty long-term business.

How should a business model change while developing disruptive innovation?

There isn't a universal answer to that question, but disruption focus is also about business model innovation. Once you define the job-to-be-done, the "what," and the value chain delivery model, the business model innovation is the architectural frame to structure your offer and is the third element of the unsettled disruption core framework.

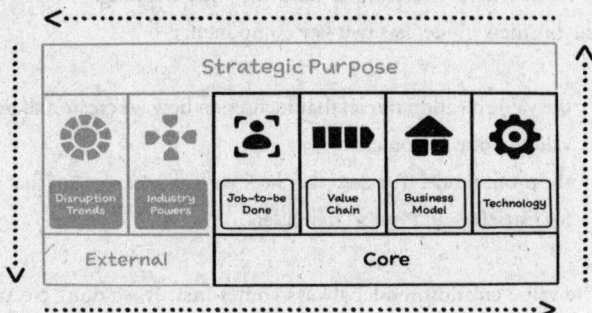

Figure 17 - Unsettled Disruption – Business Model

WHAT IS BUSINESS MODEL INNOVATION?

Haim Mendelson, Stanford GSB, the Kleiner Perkins Caufield & Byers Professor of Electronic Business and Commerce and Management [101], explains a business model as a high-level architectural plan for a home. Mendelson said, "Would you make it without putting together a blueprint first?" The business model describes your innovative product or service, the market, and the economic engine that will enable it to meet its profitability and growth objectives.

A business model enables a company to meet its set objectives, primarily by assisting in value creation for its customers, and revenue generation. Whenever a new venture is starting or an existing business is to be improved for better results, the principal objective is to discover a business model that would make a perfect fit for its key targets.

However, the value creation model becomes more prominent and takes the lead. If there is no value creation during the whole process, a company will be unable to perform. Nevertheless, if you are generating value but somehow unable to convert it into revenue, it will not be possible to retain the resources to keep the business running [102].

Even a venture designed to achieve social objectives rather than profit would require some financing to keep the wheels rolling. Keep in mind that the business model has two key components:

- the value creation model that focuses on how we create and deliver value to our customers,
- the profit model that describes how we'll extract some of that value for ourselves and our shareholders.

The value creation model always comes first. If we don't create any value, there's nothing for us to extract. But in the end, both are important because if you create a lot of value but don't manage to extract any of it, we won't have the resources to keep the business alive. In other words, Business Model Innovation is a process to create and deliver value to the customers.

THE IMPORTANCE OF BUSINESS MODEL INNOVATION

We witnessed that businesses that can't keep up with the times don't stay afloat for long. Innovation is essential, but businesses' optimal strategy to stay up to date and profitable is the strategic foundation.

Business model innovation allows a company to take advantage of changing customer demands and expectations. Organizations unable to innovate and shift their business models may be displaced by newcomers who could better meet customer needs. The recent pandemic has caused a tremendous global shift in the economy and business structures. It has challenged the conventional method of conducting business using strict reliance on traditional approaches.

Many companies have learned new ways of serving customers and creating value differently. These times have taught us to move away from the usual practices, jump out of our comfort zones, and explore new avenues. One aspect that I always discuss with customers is that disruptive innovation is not about being the first. You can apply business model innovation to answer other disruptors and still be relevant. Let's learn how this happens through real-life examples.

AMAZON, THE CONCEPT OF MARKETPLACE

In 1995, the world's biggest bookstore, Amazon, was launched [103]. Two decades later, this company revolutionized Cloud computing and paved its way to compete with various industries. Today, Amazon is not just delivering groceries to your doorsteps but also producing Emmy award-winning entertainment. The organization conquered innumerable challenges through its perseverance and innovative business model to become a trillion-dollar company.

Amazon introduced "Amazon Auctions" in 1999 as a refined e-commerce platform in competition with eBay [104]. It didn't work as expected. However, rather than discarding the initiative, Amazon remodeled it as "Amazon Marketplace," [105] merging the Amazon website with the new e-commerce platform, bringing Amazon's and its retailers' products in one place for customers.

Amazon's marketplace became bigger than Amazon itself. This disruptive business model was developed using the same customer base and products, but with a different selling approach. It serves as an example of how disruption happens by business model innovation.

ATARI, VIDEO GAME SHIFT

The industry of video games has faced several challenges in the past decade. Initially, consoles were bulky, making them inaccessible for many customers. This difficulty led to the innovation of arcades, which needed customers to have credit for playing games [106].

As technology advanced, the consoles became more compact, economical, and accessible. In particular, Atari started selling directly to customers, excluding the middle parties involved. Recent times have seen an increase in demand for accessibility of video games on smartphones. Accordingly, the game developers have gone through structural business model innovation to support this requirement.

Initially, this demand was filled by the subscription-based level upgrade. In contrast, some organizations offered free-of-charge games by charging for in-app advertising or merchandise selling. This change in the business model drastically shifted their revenue stream and customer reach simultaneously.

MARS, DIVERSIFICATION

Mars started as a candy manufacturing business by introducing chocolate-based products, including Milky Way, M&Ms, and Snickers. With time, Mars diversified its business portfolio into pet food, and later veterinary hospitals.

In early 2017, Mars acquired Veterinary Center of America [107], an institution owning 800 animal hospitals in the USA, for $7.7 billion, strengthening their footing in the pet market to the most unbreakable point.

The strategy adopted by Mars is about innovation and finding novel ways of branding their products. The company identifies its strengths and then applies them to its new products differently by implementing new business models.

HILTI, FROM SELLING TO RENTING

Hilti is a well-renowned multinational company dealing in construction, maintenance, and mining industry products. It primarily produces products that are sold to professional end-users.

Hilti's customers' understanding resulted in customers who did not need to own some of their products. Therefore, they moved from the purchase transaction model to the rental business model [108] and started renting the tools they produced to answer their customers' job-to-be-done. In 2016 Hilti had 1.5 million tools under fleet management [109].

NINTENDO WII, FROM HIGH TECH TO LOW TECH

In 2003, the profits of the Japanese game and console developer Nintendo fell by 38 percent [110]. Several major game developers pulled their support for GameCube, Nintendo's main console at the time. Nintendo's sidestep focused on an untapped market segment, "casual gamer," and released the Wii in 2006, a simplified console that targeted this massive user group.

Nintendo's new business model shifted from costly high-tech activities and resources to low-cost ones. And Nintendo sold five times more Wii than GameCube.

EASYBANK, THE BRANCHLESS SERVICES

Easybank [111] is the second-largest direct bank of Austria. It offers a wide range of online and branchless financial products. Since there is minimal need for physical branches for customer interaction, infrastructure and maintenance are very low. Consequently, they can waive off transaction fees and account charges, disrupting the traditional banking service industry.

BUSINESS MODEL INNOVATION AND DISRUPTION

Business model innovation is a strategic part of the innovation process. It is not as simple as changing a policy or understanding market patterns. Further, since every business is unique, it isn't easy to pick the right approach and strategy out of the numerous options available. There are endless variables to be taken into consideration while innovating an existing business model. Preparing for this challenging task and finding the right equation is the only way forward in this process.

We can classify business models in several ways. For instance, they are based on how companies and startups monetize their business, how they deal with their suppliers and customers, and the value proposition which those companies can offer to several stakeholders. In some cases such as Microsoft or Amazon, there isn't a single way to describe a business model. Some companies have diversified their operations so much that they can generate multiple value propositions across several stakeholders and industries.

Uncertainty is an undeniable element in the process. When we take the road of disruptive innovation, we are only trying a pattern we never tried before. We will end up making mistakes while experimenting. Now we will explore eight innovative business models. This is not an extensive list, but it will help you to imagine your next move.

1. FREE

This model is also referred to as the "if-you're-not-paying-for-the-product-you-are-the-product" model [112]. It is a model where the end consumer is the product itself by serving as an "advertising eyeball" for the company. This way, the service becomes free of charge. Revenue could be generated through advertising played while using platforms, such as Facebook, Twitter, or Google.

Twitter is monetizing its users' attention in two ways: advertising, and data licensing. In 2020 with total revenue of $3.72 billion [113], advertising represented 86.5 percent of its revenue, and data licensing at 13.5 percent, primarily related to enterprise clients using data for their analyses [114].

2. FREEMIUM

Freemium [100] is the most frequently used business model among those online products that have maximum demand for essential functions.

This model helps build a customer base through free services, and slowly a larger clientele is built by creating product association. Free can be a powerful weapon for growth.

Once the customers are hooked to using the service, the service supplier starts charging for premium services. This model is also known as disruption through digital sampling. It works perfectly well where the marginal cost for extra units and distribution is lower than advertising revenue or personal data sale. Some successful examples of this model are Dropbox, Spotify, Skype, and Zoom. They offer a set of basic features for free and premium services at different rates.

Spotify is a music streaming platform that gives users access to an extensive catalog of music. It uses a freemium revenue model that offers a basic, limited, ad-supported service for free, and an unlimited premium service for a subscription fee. Spotify relies heavily on its music algorithms and its community of users and artists to maintain its optimal premium experience. Its premium subscriber base has grown from 10 percent of total users in 2011 to 45 percent in 2021 [115] representing 155 million premium subscribers and 345 million monthly active users.

3. SUBSCRIPTION

Using the subscription model, you charge once for products or services delivered for a specific period, or split the fee into periodic payments. The main objective here is to get the customer on board for a longer time. It ensures that customer enjoys product improvement and extension as well throughout the relationship.

For instance, Netflix, Dollar Shave Club (DSC), and companies like Peloton[116] are using this model. They are innovating by "locking in" the customer for an extended period rather than with an ad hoc purchase. The first-time customer makes a purchase and becomes a conversion into a repeat customer through subscription.

In 2012, DSC launched its online store and quickly disrupted the overpriced men's razor blade market. It purchased its products from wholesalers, removed the traditional physical retail channel, and sold razors and blades online at a lower price.

The Dollar Shave Club captures value by employing low-cost economics and a monthly or bi-monthly subscription model that promotes customer stickiness. In 2015, with 4 million subscribers, Dollar Shave claimed 48.6 percent of the online razor market, shaking giants Gillette and Schick [19]. Unilever acquired the company in 2016 for approximately $1 billion [117].

4. MARKETPLACE

This disruptive business model brings buyers and sellers together at one platform, and in return, charges a nominal fee or commission. The revenue is generated through this commission or fixed transaction costs. Once the platform starts pulling traffic, it brings in another revenue stream by adding advertising. For instance, some of the leading players who have laid the foundation of this model are Amazon Marketplace, eBay, and Uber.

Another example is the Alibaba Group, the largest e-commerce retail company in the world. They are producing absolutely no product themselves and hence have no inventory. Alibaba's primary mission relies on bringing together Chinese sellers with buyers from around the world at one platform to purchase every kind of product.

The value created by Alibaba is through the software interface, not in the products themselves. For the twelve months ending 31 December 2020, Alibaba revenue was $93.884 billion, a 32.13 percent increase year-over-year [118]. As of March 2020, annual active consumers for the Alibaba Digital Economy reached 960 million globally, including 780 million consumers in China and 180 million consumers outside China [119].

5. SHARING ECONOMY

The previously well-known business of renting has now taken the shape of a sharing economy model. Merchandise that can't be purchased is made available to potential customers for a limited period of time. This model can be applied to any product, whether from individuals or businesses, real estate, or even intangible goods.

A relevant prime example is carpooling. Consider Getaround, where a vehicle is allotted to a customer for a certain period and kilometers against a specific fee. We can also mention Airbnb, enabling people to list, find, and rent accommodations against a processing fee. Airbnb doesn't rent a space from the host. Instead, it only lets the host share its specifications on the Airbnb portal for someone who might be looking for a place to rent. Their business model builds on the sharing economy and believes that house owners are willing to rent unused space to strangers for passive income.

The success of Airbnb's business model is based on a resource-light cost structure. It found an innovative way to partner with idle asset (empty rooms) owners and help them monetize those assets via their matchmaking platform.

As of September 2020, four million hosts offer Airbnb services across 100,000 cities and more than 800 million Airbnb guest arrivals. Host average annual earning represents $7,900 [120].

Airbnb differs from other matchmaking sites like booking.com or hotels.com in that travelers associate the listed properties and rooms with the Airbnb brand as if it was a traditional hotel chain.

6. USER EXPERIENCE PREMIUM

First-class brands adopt this model by creating an extraordinary service experience for the customers and charging premium prices. Apple, Tesla, and many other top-quality brands are using this model [121].

Premium makes a product with perceived higher customer value or an unmatchable service and charges extra money against it. Customers happily pay a premium for such products and services as they perceive the value extracted from them as very high in terms of experience.

Tesla creates electric cars that are easy and uncomplicated. The positive experience leads to customers endorsing the Tesla brand to their social circle. Nine out of ten Tesla customers recommend their car to their friends and family to support this premium service [122]. Tesla makes considerable investments in its infrastructure to enhance its growth.

In March 2020, Tesla passed the $600 billion market capitalization, becoming the world's ninth most valuable company by market cap [123].

7. ECOSYSTEM

This model creates consumer dependency by linking customers to an ecosystem through a "locking in" system.

An ecosystem model [124] has disrupted industries by selling an interdependent suite of products and services that increase in value as you buy in bulk. For example, both iOS and Android have created an ecosystem where customers are bound to make purchases that will sync with their existing system. The issue of compatibility locks in the customers, making it difficult for them to churn to another brand.

The difficulty in churning also creates a barrier for competitors to steal the foothold of an existing player. It allows only Apple or Google to wield enormous power in the end-to-end supply chain.

8. DONATION-BASED MODEL

The concept of this model is when an organization gets most of its funds in the form of donations from individuals and corporations worldwide.

Wikipedia, the online encyclopedia that helps improve your general knowledge, is free of cost. It is an open-source platform where innumerable online contributors share their information without any financial gain, and their model is based on user donations.

This makes the Wikipedia business model reasonably easy to understand. The organization only focuses on handling the website, servers, and administration, and the volunteers contribute the main content for free. Wikipedia operates on a donation-based revenue model where it gets most of its funds in donations from individuals and corporations around the world.

In 2020, Wikipedia has more than 41 million users who have registered a username. Only 143,000 users regularly contribute [125]. According to its annual report, Wikipedia earned total revenue of over $109 million in 2020, but none of it came from advertisements, affiliates, or any paid service [126].

LEVERAGING DIGITIZATION TO SCALE TRACTION

Business models in the era dominated by digital platforms have taught us that competitive advantages are outside the company's boundaries. Businesses must know how to take advantage of those external resources, making competition more fluid, unpredictable, and hard to build using an old business playbook.

Therefore, tech giant companies like Amazon have learned to take advantage of network effects. Instead of following a linear logic, such business models have built-in flywheels focused on customer obsessions. Hence, the point to be noted is that you need to realize that the internet and digital era have devised several new ways of doing business. Integrated with digital platforms, new business models require a reformed playbook altogether.

TECHNOLOGICAL INNOVATION VS. BUSINESS MODEL INNOVATION

Business model innovation is about expanding the perimeters of success of an organization using existing products and technologies. By aiming to craft a compelling value proposition, it propels the business model to multiply its customer base and develop a lasting competitive advantage.

However, technological advancements have pushed towards alternative approaches to doing business. For instance, innovative business models of companies like Netflix, Airbnb, or Zoom would not be possible if technology didn't allow new ways of delivering content, sharing and connecting. Thus, we must remember that technological innovation is completely different from business innovation because it happens in labs or research centers instead of in a business context.

Technological innovation requires many upfront resources and researchers, and it might not follow business objectives as it experiments freely with ideas that take time to work out.

Technology alone does not become a competitive advantage; it has to be added up with other elements, including but not limited to new ideas of serving customers, developing a robust distribution network, as well as monetizing techniques.

Therefore, any entrepreneur or innovator who develops a business model must design its multiple variations to test those in the market. Thus, the prime objective is to find the product-market fit.

TAKEAWAYS

Business model innovation is the third element of the core of unsettled disruption. It represents the high-level architectural plan for your disruptive innovation, as it describes your innovative product or service, the market, and the economic engine that will enable you to meet its profitability and growth objectives.

The recent pandemic has caused a tremendous global shift in the economy and businesses' structures. It has made us question the conventional method of conducting business, and has eased management on strict reliance on traditional approaches. Many companies have learned new ways of serving customers and creating value differently. These times have taught us to move away from the usual practices, jump out of our comfort zones, and explore new avenues.

Now is the time to learn from the examples of leading business models. In the embryonic phase of a project, we should start by testing various business models and learning approaches. It is also called trial and error. This process of discovery has an element of uncertainty and risk.

This uncertainty can be handled by focusing on testing low-resolution prototypes as an experiment. Once your approach with one customer is evaluated, the validated hypothesis supports refining the problem statement, and the testing loop is repeated. Only after successful trials, you scale up and expand.

At this moment, you probably feel inspired by a lot of new ideas at each step of the process. In the next chapter, we will explore the last pillar of the unsettled disruption core framework, "technology," and learn how to leverage it as a disruption enabler.

CHAPTER 10
TECHNOLOGY AS DISRUPTION ENABLER

"Technology gives us power, but it does not and cannot tell us how to use that power. Thanks to technology, we can instantly communicate across the world, but it still doesn't help us know what to say."
Jonathan Sacks

I REMEMBER MEETING THE innovation director of one of the world's biggest banks around twelve years ago. He came to us to identify new trends, the potential of disruption, and ways to prioritize the bank's innovation strategy. After an hour of discussion, I realized they hadn't disrupted themselves; instead, they have only used technology to offer online services with the same old restrictions of in-branch services. His company provided a mobile wallet that required the users to visit their branch for activation. He was wondering about the low user penetration.

Although he had a whole team dedicated to working on new technologies, which gave him extra confidence in their services, he didn't feel threatened by new entrants. If we look at it now, banks are in a questionable position. Some experts have highlighted that banks will no longer be needed in the coming years and might cease to exist. This can be attributed to continually developing financial technology (fintech) that has entirely changed the global financial markets' face.

Most financial services have been digitized and are available through payment apps, mobile wallets, and robo-advisors [127]. Disruptors utilize new technologies to improve the current system, identify and fulfill the jobs-to-be-done, stream the value chain, and propose innovative business models.

But why? The challenge wasn't about technology, but people were looking for better services to improve their personal and work-life quality. In some countries, they were looking to access financial services which had been impossible because of the distance and the cost to get to the branch office for any transaction.

It's not hard to realize that these fintech companies cannot enhance the banking sector; instead, they disrupt the current market; they have emerged as serious competitors. Newcomers have been leveraging technology, offering better services, payment methods, currency exchanging options, online lending, crowdfunding, and wealth management facilities, giving traditional banks and other financial institutions a hard time.

Some of them are applying the disruption principles, starting with the underserved market, and then going upstream. Their core focus is a problem-solver targeting an underserved market niche by combining all disruption pillars.

Then financial institutions started taking a new approach; many had invested in business accelerators to speed-up fintech. As a result, the banking sector has adopted these programs to address disruptive threats and engage with financial startups.

IS TECHNOLOGY A DISRUPTION ENABLER OR A MEANS TO IT?

The prime factor behind the success or failure of a so-called disruption lies in answering this question. When planning to disrupt, businesses need to know that technology can only aid in disruption and is not its sole requisite. Companies often invest a large chunk of their resources into finding ways to use technology without looking into the problem they want to solve. Thus, they end up investing in the wrong segment of the market, which might allow them to make some profit, but that does not make them disruptors.

Therefore, companies that analyze technology's role in disruption before investing in it have a high chance of skyrocketing their business to unimaginable heights. However, the businesses that prefer risking their resources before finding the real problem may end up empty-handed.

So, technology comes as the fourth phase of the unsettled disruption core as an innovation enabler.

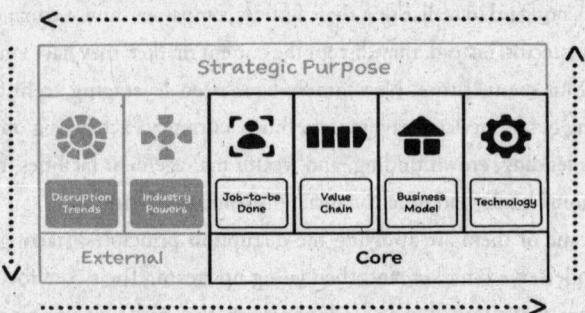

Figure 18 - Unsettled Disruption - Technology

WHAT HOLDS THE POTENTIAL FOR DISRUPTION?

I cannot emphasize enough the importance of technology for disruption. However, the factor that makes any technology fruitful is its proper use. I cross paths with many people who wish to establish a company with just the idea of utilizing new technology.

They'd straight out ask me if they should start a new business, but only because they think Artificial Intelligence or Blockchain is the next big thing. My answer is always a counter-question: which problem are you solving, and how are you enabling it?

ADDRESSING THE PROBLEM

Finding solutions without real problems only leads to wasting precious resources. Let's recall the disruptive innovation definition as the emergence of new businesses dedicated to serving a portion of the audience left unanswered by the market leaders [14]. In others words to focus on an unanswered market segment and problem.

To disrupt a market or industry, you need to figure out the unfulfilled "jobs-to-be-done." The specific features satisfying those requirements will add value to your product, thus motivating the market to leave the previous products and try out yours. Thus, all technology, resources, and dreams to disrupt the industry will go down the drain if your end product or service does not deliver value to the customers.

THREE EXAMPLES OF TECHNOLOGY AS A DISRUPTION ENABLER

Technology like highly advanced microprocessors, artificial intelligence, and connectivity, just to mention a few, is what forms the core enablers of disruptive business structures. Businesses undergo substantial supply and value chain changes, scope transformation, and cultural shake with these powerful enablers, which set them apart from other industry leaders.

Rapid technological development facilitates businesses in improving the production and distribution process, helping them invest and focus on their customers' quality, enhancing users' experience like Skype, eBay, and Wikipedia did. Consequently, ideas are turning into end products faster than ever. Such scenarios have blurred the line between contributors including producers, wholesalers, retailers, etc., because of the unconventional activities that technology could enable.

Nowadays, even the whole process of testing an idea could be reduced to a landing page online, which is many times quicker and cost-effective than developing a physical product and testing its response. These technological advancements allow companies to target a smaller market with a specific issue while making enough profit. They can quickly start with the limited capital and human force required to serve the small market, unlike the days when businesses could only begin with a massive investment.

The next examples explain how these companies leveraged technology to deliver value and become industry leaders.

EBAY

The launch of eBay disrupted the local second-hand and retailers market. Although the need for used items existed at the time and auctions were not a new idea, the way it was delivered was to change the industry.

eBay [128] anchored technology gave rise to disruption. Web-based second-hand selling and auctions were a twist in the current market that people could not resist. Convenience, ease, and comfort have always been the prime factor of a product's success, and eBay came with a lot more. It allowed people to purchase and sell without geographical boundaries—all over the globe. Then, it offered PayPal, which further simplified the trading process [129].

It is a great example of how technology can be a disruption enabler but not a means. The core of eBay's value was to connect sellers and buyers through a trusted platform that enables this secure exchange.

Due to consistent technological advancements, industries are witnessing frequent disruptions because businesses can fulfill various market requirements, increasing almost parallel to the tech. In 2020, eBay connected more than 183 million buyers on their marketplace, operating in 190 markets [128].

SKYPE

Remember when we needed telephone and mobile cards to make local and international phone calls back in the day? Telcos used to charge per minute, which was both expensive and inconvenient. Due to the high cost, people often had to wait for hours to discuss everything over a single call. Their availability was another issue. Running out of credit over long calls was a common problem and was more annoying than anything else, as we had to go out to buy cards each time, which was quite frequent. Things would get worse in emergencies.

When Skype came out, it disrupted these telecommunication companies by allowing end-users to communicate online for free. The Skype business model was possible thanks to P2P computing techniques and voice over-internet protocol establishing a new communication standard [130]. Skype set the foundation for the industry's disruption, which was later populated by many other applications like Messenger and WhatsApp. Today, when we have so many applications to make free calls online to anyone in any part of the world, it's extremely unlikely for anyone to make use of traditional phone calls, especially for international dealings.

The telecommunication companies saw their market share and revenue evaporate into thin air, with heavy hearts. People preferred Skype because of the convenience it offered. The disruptor focused on developing a user-friendly interface for customers, enabling them to get used to it in minutes. In March 2020, Skype was used by 100 million people every month and by 40 million people daily [131].

WIKIPEDIA

Wikipedia is another example of a disruptor that started on a small scale but was able to expand massively by leveraging technology.

Back in the old days, parents used to buy giant encyclopedias so their kids could excel in each subject at school. It was challenging to ensure their children had the best academic books they could afford. Encyclopedia sellers used to come to our houses, offering the primary source of knowledge at home. This otherwise necessitated going to the library, which was not a last-minute thing to do as it required some planning. Once we finally got one encyclopedia at home, we had to be extremely careful with each book's page, as they cost no less than a fortune. Well, gone are those days.

Therefore, knowledge is much more widely accessible nowadays. During the '90s, Microsoft launched Encyclopedia for computers that took over almost half of Britannica's business—the traditional encyclopedia. Then in 2000, Wikipedia changed the rules of the encyclopedia market game. It was different from Microsoft's and Britannica's working model because it offered better availability of content to the general audience [132].

Wikipedia came out as an open-source educational website that provided user-based content. It was available to everyone online, which further enhanced its demand and success. Another main reason behind Wikipedia's success was its ability to let users enjoy a free treasure chest of content. It solved a job-to-be-done and exchanged the value chain and business model by using technology. After its launch, people opted for the more convenient and free content source.

According to Wikimedia Statistics [133], in December 2020, Wikipedia has recorded more than 22.3 billion page views and it is ranked among the most visited sites globally, according to Alexa [134].

TAKEAWAYS

Looking into the technology as an enabler to create value is the last element of the core of the unsettled disruption framework. When planning to disrupt, businesses need to know that technology can only aid in disruption and is not its sole requisite. Companies often invest a large chunk of their resources into finding ways to use technology without looking into the problem they want to solve.

You can start by tracking back and determining technologies' ability to help you disrupt your market. It is fundamental to understand their work and identify how you can use it to deliver value to the customers. With Skype, eBay, and Wikipedia, it's obvious that disruption requires the need created by an unfilled job. With the proper use of technology, these companies could make the offering accessible to a broader audience with a better value.

For anybody planning to disrupt the market, there are tons of opportunities out there. It would be best to recognize them, find out the right technology for it, and use the unsettled disruption framework to define the what and the how before onboarding into technology specifications.

Therefore, companies that analyze technology's role in disruption before investing in it have a high chance of skyrocketing their business. However, the businesses that prefer risking their resources before finding the real problem may end up with a collection of unused patents.

Now, you are ready to move onwards to Part III of this book, where we will learn from several companies' experiences, how they unsettled disruption, and how the framework applies. We will also discuss why some others missed the disruption mark.

The following chapters will be a source of inspiration by exploring incumbents' self-disruption, then analyzing the new disruptors' model, moving towards companies that fail disruption, and studying disruptors that flourished during the 2020 pandemic.

PART III
PROVEN EXPERIENCE

CHAPTER 11
INCUMBENTS CAME OUT STRONGER VIA SELF-DISRUPTION

"If you always do what you always did, you will always get what you always got."
Albert Einstein

IN 2007, I WAS in charge of building the three-year strategic plan for a company that boasted double-digit growth for more than ten years, thanks to its hardware solutions. The technology in question was getting commoditized by Chinese manufacturers. Soon, the trends changed and favored an approach dominated by software. Sounds familiar? Many industries have been affected by digitalization, and this is not going to stop any time soon.

The strategic challenge was how to prepare for such disruptive sources while protecting the company's position, revenue, and brand. This transformation should be combined with an understanding of the ecosystem and in-depth analysis of customer "jobs-to-be-done," value chain, and business models. Accomplishing this change of focusing on a big structure wasn't easy and took nearly ten years of continuous evolution, including mergers, acquisitions, cultural struggles, and strategic partnerships.

It's believed that small companies are more adept at carrying out disruptive innovation. These start-ups are risk-takers with low overhead costs to fund their innovative styles. Moreover, they can reinvent and re-orient themselves quickly.

CEOs of incumbents typically fail to innovate when the main challenges are related to adopting change. Despite this norm, some existing giants have welcomed disruptive innovation with open arms and then succeeded in self-disruption.

WHO OR WHAT IS AN INCUMBENT?

Let's start by defining an incumbent. An incumbent is an established entity with a dominant position in its respective industry. Examples in this chapter include such companies as Microsoft, LEGO, and Disney.

The initiation phase of disruption may not challenge such incumbents; however, underestimating the importance for long may result in catastrophic downfalls. Self-disruption may seem strange, but it is the best way to survive evolving times for organizations. The mindset that adapting to change will affect an entity's core business is myopic at best. Let's look at how these incumbents embraced and survived the disruptive innovation onslaught.

MICROSOFT—SELF-DISRUPTION FOR SUCCESS

The creator of MS-DOS, Microsoft, whose software became ubiquitous in daily life, was faced with market disruption. Despite Microsoft staying ahead in OS development, competitors turned to Cloud-based computing. The era of Windows devices as the sole operating system was overturned as Google, Amazon, and Salesforce entered the fray. The new age of multiple environments and devices was upon us.

Through the appointment of a new CEO in 2014, Satya Nadella changed Microsoft's mindset altogether and its culture for the better. As noted in his book [135] *Hit Refresh,* his focus was "Transformation through a sense of empathy to empower others."

HOW DID MICROSOFT HIT A REFRESH?

A company like Microsoft, which was in the industry for over two decades, sees plenty of resistance to change. Maturity thus becomes a stumbling block for many as deep-rooted traits and habits are set in stone. However, Microsoft transformed itself into a provider of IT solutions instead of just selling the Windows experience.

In his book [135], Nadella stressed that defining a clear sense of purpose and identity was the first step to achieve success. They also needed a strong understanding of how to express this purpose and implement a business transforming strategy. Microsoft adapted to the changing trends by not resting on its laurels and brand power. It paid close attention to its customers' needs instead of churning out the same recipes for development [136].

The company made a name for itself selling a package of software that became ingrained in their ethos. However, Microsoft realigned by realizing that its traditional linkages could be nurtured to sell IT solutions to corporate clients. Thus, they became the enabler for such organizations to embrace Cloud-based computing services.

Microsoft achieved the change of its mindset and culture by aligning the available resources to a new business model. The company started a subscription-based service by offering paid services to its customers who were updated regularly.

Also, Microsoft changed their view about competitors who were then seen as potential partners and even used as a way to enhance its offering. Examples of this mindset change include partnering with companies such as Amazon, Apple, and Red Hat [137].

Since the appointment of Satya Nadella as CEO of Microsoft, the traditional tech giant has been transformed into a leader in Cloud services. This embrace of innovation sees a nod of approval from investors whose confidence in the company is exemplified by its market value exceeding $1 trillion, one of just a handful in history to hit that mark. When Nadella first took over, its market value was around $300 billion [136].

LEGO—LESS IS MORE

LEGO has been a big name in the construction toys for children industry. For the parents out there, LEGO is still one of the best distractions over screen addiction. A success spanning decades saw a change in fortunes at the start of the millennia.

LEGO is well aware of being on the wrong side of innovation. During the 1990s, LEGO diversified its portfolio and invested in food, clothing, video games, and even theme parks. All these ventures saw losses. Then, LEGO retired its long-serving designers, the newer recruits brought complicated designs, and the company was near bankruptcy. Despite these new ventures, the company was in hot water as the CEO expressed in a statement: "We're on a burning platform... and probably won't survive [138]."

HOW DID LEGO RETURN TO PROFITABILITY?

A significant change in fortunes occurred when LEGO released its first movie in 2014 [139]. The film wasn't a mere marketing ploy, because it grew a following of its own. The movie was a modern epic that captured the imagination of kids and adults alike. The film galvanized support for the LEGO company as a creator of unique and creative projects. Thus, by self-disrupting their business to a new sector, LEGO became once again an instantly recognizable brand name in its core business.

LEGO went back to what it was known for: simplicity in design, few color offerings, and less third-party tie-ins. It dropped the meddling in various niches and looked to harness the customer feedback for its product improvement. A social media presence in this regard also helped the product get positive reviews from fans.

LEGO strengthened its basics by going back to its roots "job-to-be-done." The brand amplified the user experience through social and film media. LEGO doesn't merely represent a product but a lifestyle, an environment that users get to enjoy and feel. The LEGO experience is centered around a premium, intuitive, and highly coveted product that fans adore.

DISNEY—IMPENDING DISRUPTION

The coronavirus pandemic crippled Disney's media empire—except for some major success: Disney+. Disney+ was launched in November 2019 for $6.99 a month, and couldn't have come at a better time for Disney. It has seen remarkable growth, with 60 million subscribers by August 2020 [140].

Bob Iger, CEO of Disney, realized straightaway when licensing Disney's library for Netflix that they would soon be its biggest rival. By 2017, Disney stopped its licensing to Netflix to create its own streaming platform [141]. Among other media channels such as CBS and Apple, Disney was the first to realize this goldmine's potential.

HOW DID THEY DECIDE TO DISRUPT THEIR BUSINESS MODEL?

Iger's success can be attributed to the pursuit of three strategies: disrupting their value chain and offering by embracing technology; keeping customer closeness via a direct channel; and beefing up Disney to make it a giant in the field.

As described in *The New York Times* article in September 2019 [142], Iger's first masterstroke was to reconcile with Steve Jobs, Pixar's owner, which subsequently laid the foundation for Pixar's acquisition later in the same year for $7.4 billion. Because content is the principal value asset for Disney, it furthered its agenda by acquiring Lucas Films for $4 billion (2013) and Marvel Studios for $4.24 billion (2009).

Netflix was overtaking by 2015, leading Robert A. Iger to test a streaming app in Great Britain. By 2016, the Disney CEO was hinting at building a similar platform to rival Netflix. The idea seemed like a risky one, especially for a traditional giant such as Disney, with its roots deeply entrenched in the television industry. By 2017, the conventional TV numbers were suffering, which led to the increased pace of launching streaming services such as ESPN+ for sports and Disney+ for all the blockbuster movies.

Disney's strategic preference for disruption was demonstrated through Pixar's acquisition and the restoration of Disney Imagineers. It was further enhanced by acquiring BAMtech, streaming technology, and finally, the launch of Disney+ in November 2019 [142]. Since 2005, Iger has understood the impending disruption of the media industry. The Iger lesson: Disrupt yourself before someone else does it.

TAKEAWAYS

It is believed that incumbents typically fail to innovate when the main challenges are related to adopting change. Despite this norm, some incumbents have welcomed disruptive innovation with open arms and succeeded in self-disruption. We learned the importance of seeing your company and products with a fresh pair of eyes. So, when you think of "disruptive innovation," don't look at your competitors because they're not going to disrupt you.

Use unsettled disruption by being aware of the disruption trends, especially now that systems are changing quickly. The strategic challenge should be how to combine this understanding of the ecosystem and competitive position with the in-depth analysis of customer "jobs-to-be-done," value chain, business models, and technology and aligned with your strategic purpose.

Customers are always looking for better services; hence they are not looking for competitors but an improved user experience. By embracing disruption as a positive force, you can increase customers' utility and build a better organization for the future.

In a nutshell: Use unsettled disruption as an opportunity to grow stronger, or watch your business die. In the next chapter, we will discover how a new generation of disruptors are changing the market even more quickly.

CHAPTER 12
NEW DISRUPTORS' GENERATION

"If you can visualize it, if you can dream it, there's some way to do it."
Walt Disney

WOULD YOU BELIEVE THAT Airbnb started one of the significant disruption journeys because its owners could not pay their rent? Airbnb's owners wanted to earn some extra cash; thus, they rented three of their mattresses in a San Francisco apartment. One could not imagine how such a small step could evolve into such a massive disruption. Airbnb opened the door for new businesses. With no investment in setting up its infrastructure, Airbnb found a formula to stream the value chain and reduce operating costs.

Note that initially, these disruptors such as Airbnb or Netflix did not have a significant offering. Instead, they were low-cost, and favorable for only a small market segment, leaving the larger portion of the market unaffected. Due to their primary offering and small market share, they did not appear to threaten the incumbents. Consequently, the incumbents continued to center their attention on improving their existing products and services for their current market instead of looking beyond that. Their ignorance towards the new entrants ultimately formed the basis of the new guys' success.

In a March 2014 *Fast Company* article, the EVP of Four Seasons said [143], "Our guests don't want the Airbnb feel and scent. Airbnb doesn't really compete with the Four Seasons because its amateur hosts can't match the level of hospitality this hotel's professional concierges offer, and its customers expect."

However, there is a new trend; the new generation of disruptors are becoming more aggressive with unique products and services that target the unattended market sector and appeal to incumbents' loyal customers since the beginning. In this new generation, we see an evolving path of the disruption concept and a difference in disruptive approaches to previous and current disruptors.

CHANGING DISRUPTORS' PROFILE—THE NEW GENERATION

The MIT Sloan Management Review article "The New Disrupters" [144] has highlighted the dramatic changes in disruptors' profiles in recent years. Disruptors like Netflix and Airbnb started with low-quality and inferior products, but the new disruptors are marching in with high-quality, convenient, and affordable products, making it extremely challenging for the incumbents to cope.

Warby Parker and Canva are two examples of this new generation. Unlike Airbnb, they directly targeted the entry points of their specific industries. With these new disruptors, we notice how the core of the industry's business, not a niche segment, is their primary target. They identify the market's unfulfilled segment and provide them with superior products that ultimately reach out to the leading segments quickly.

New generation disruptors succeed by conducting an in-depth analysis of ways to stream their value chain and redefine their business models using modern technologies that others haven't utilized effectively. The innovative use of technologies and unconventional strategies crushes the incumbents like never before. The disruptors offer cost-effective and similar or even better features to the customers, alongside mitigating almost all frictional factors associated with conventional products and services.

WARBY PARKER AND HOW THEY DISRUPTED THE EYEWEAR INDUSTRY

With a net worth of about $138.7 billion in 2019 [145], the eyewear industry was under Luxottica's strict monopoly. This company owned almost all eyewear brands, including Ray-Ban, Persol, Pearl Vision, Oakley, and one of the largest vision insurance companies in the US, the EyeMed.

THE ENTRY POINT—JOB-TO-BE-DONE

Before becoming the co-founder of Warby Parker, Dave Gilboa worked at Wharton computer lab and had a hobby of complaining about glasses. One day at work, he mentioned to two of his friends, Neil and Andrew, how he lost his glasses while backpacking for a trip and had to buy another, which cost him $600, more than his brand-new iPhone [146].

As described in the company story, the three friends were taken aback by how unnecessarily expensive the glasses were in those days. Another friend soon joined them, and the conversation turned into a full-fledged business idea. They aimed at disrupting a market where glasses cost more than an iPhone, and everyday people could not afford to wear them, let alone own multiple pairs.

Today, Warby Parker is among the leading eyewear brands that offer affordable glasses starting at $95 [147].

VALUE CHAIN

The founders of Warby Parker realized that cutting prices would require cutting the costs. They intended to bring down prices while providing quality products.

Hence, they came up with a low-cost business structure without licensing fees and middleman expenses. They focused on streaming the value chain by designing their frames, sourcing their raw material, and directly working with the manufacturers. The frames were made in China and delivered to the US through an external logistics firm. The rest of the process is conducted at local labs [148].

BUSINESS MODEL

Warby's redefined business model enabled it to cut down the prices and sold lensed glasses at less than $100 [149]. They decided to sell directly to the end-users through their website, which allowed them to propose better prices and build healthy, close relationships with their customers. Direct feedback from the clients gave them a chance to improve their product and service.

THE EXPERIENCE

Warby Parker allows users to try the glasses before placing an order. Customers can select up to five frames to receive in the mail and keep for five days to try them [150]. Once the trial is over, they must return the frames and place the order for their selections. What's more, the customers can return or exchange the glasses within 30 days of purchase if they are dissatisfied. In any such case, the buyer does not have to bear any shipping cost.

TECHNOLOGY

The brand depended on eCommerce to manage its value chain from the very beginning. It utilized data analysis for improved customer experience, product design, and services. It uses various online tests with VR, AI, Augmented Reality, and other technologies to ensure smooth and efficient remote eyewear shopping. In 2019, the brand introduced an online try-on facility based on Augmented Reality [151]. The feature allows customers to check how the selected eyewear looks on their faces.

THE INCUMBENT'S DRAWBACKS THAT CONTRIBUTED TO THE DISRUPTION

The eyewear industry had an oligopolistic structure, with Luxottica in a profitable position, a position the company did not want to lose. That was the biggest reason why the company did not cannibalize its own offer and continued to work with the same profit margin.

Luxottica also overlooked consumer requirements and behavior. People had long before shifted to online purchases for almost everything from accessories to raw material: so, why not glasses? As incumbent, they refrained from investing in eCommerce and other virtual features for fear of disturbing the relationships with existing value chain partners and their vested interests.

Although going online was not the only thing Luxottica needed to do, several fractional factors could be overcome to improve sales, which Warby later did—for instance, the virtual tester and the mailing service. Moreover, Luxottica's expensive eyeglasses were unaffordable for a larger market. It gave Warby a broad target market. Luxottica also overlooked the fashion trends that encouraged people to have more than one pair of glasses, because the expense prohibited most people from having more than one pair at a time.

WARBY'S PURPOSE—DO GOOD

Warby Parker was established with the mission to provide branded eyewear at low prices while laying the foundation for socially responsive businesses.

Furthermore, the brand has partnered with non-profit organization Vision Spring to actively donate one pair of glasses with each paid sale, to make them more accessible. Consequently, through their "Buy a pair, give a pair" [152] program, as of 2019, they reached out to and helped over 7 million needy people. [153]

WHAT'S NEXT

In 2019, Warby had more than 2,500 employees with 105 retail locations all over the US and Canada [153], along with its own virtual space. In August 2020, the optical giant declared closing a $245 million funding round. According to a TechCrunch 2020 report [154], it has reached a value of about $3 billion.

CANVA DESIGNS FOR EVERYONE

Canva's CEO, Melanie Perkins, wanted to enable people to create stunning designs with greater convenience and less friction [155]. That dream is a reality today. The Australian-based company, Canva, started with a clear purpose with the motto "Designs for everyone," which people didn't believe. Today, Canva has disrupted digital design as a leading graphic design platform, used by millions to create social media graphics, presentations, and other visual content.

THE ENTRY POINT—JOB-TO-BE-DONE

The founders of Canva identified the need for a platform with increasing internet marketing, specifically, blogging and social media, that requires attractive designs to gain an audience. Canva targeted this unserved market segment that included everyone who wanted to create personal designs but didn't know how. Professional designers and Adobe experts were not their buyers at this time.

However, they realized that a large segment of the market either does not know how to design, cannot afford design software, or does not have the budget to hire a designer. A survey involving 500 small-to-medium firm owners in the US concluded that 78 percent of the participants reported that non-professionals created social media graphics, presentations, and other media-related marketing content [155].

COVID-19 also fueled the platform's development, as more and more organizations were looking to get better graphics content at lower costs. Other factors that favored their growth during the pandemic are the features that allow for teamwork and improve collaboration.

VALUE CHAIN

By eliminating several steps in the process and reducing end-user dependency on intermediaries, Canva disrupted the value chain. They made it simple because the "do it yourself" model was at the core of their development, as well as integrating other services that reduced cost and provided a better user experience, such as photo libraries and other Cloud services.

CUSTOMER EXPERIENCE

The two gigantic graphic libraries—Pexels and Pixabay—are Canva's biggest customer hooks. These libraries enable Canva to deliver high-quality media to its users in need. That's what keeps its customers not only involved but also loyal.

THE BUSINESS MODEL

Since Canva wanted to stay affordable and profitable, it introduced two versions—the free and the premium. The free version offers limited images and videos; all of them are of high quality. This was an excellent driver of growth, attracting users for several segments. However, the paid or premium version offers unlimited designs.

It also offered a middle ground for people who didn't want a full subscription and could buy each design for $1 [156]. Moreover, they have a free user plan for nonprofit organizations.

Other revenue-generating offerings include Canva Print that allows printing physical graphics, Design School, and the marketplace.

The company is recently working on an offering dedicated to employees and businesses called "Canva for Work." It seeks to facilitate professional teams in collaborating to create designs.

TECHNOLOGY

Canva is a Cloud-based application that provides customers with a smooth and swift designing experience. It allows users to pick or create a style, adjust fonts and images, create videos, and much more with exceptional convenience. It hardly takes a few minutes to download and publish the designs.

CANVA PURPOSE—BEING A FORCE FOR GOOD

One of their core values at Canva, as described on their website, is "Being a force for good," which means that they are actively working towards a world that isn't just good for a few but one that's good for everyone [157]. While Canva is working with many businesses or customers, it also supports charitable organizations by offering free subscriptions to 25,000 nonprofit organizations [158].

WHAT'S NEXT

Melanie Perkins, Canva's founder, believes that her company has only achieved 1 percent of its capabilities [159]. She is looking forward to finding ways to expand her organization to widen its scope and coverage. She believes that her business can overtake many other companies to gain an ecosystem business model. As an example, Canva has recently set its sights on the education industry.

The company has witnessed a market value spike in recent years; its capital has been raised, which increased its net worth to $6 billion [160]. Canva has become an integral part of over 500,000 businesses all over the globe. It has also recorded remarkable growth in the nonprofit and educational sectors. As of October 2020, it has noted over 30 million monthly users [161].

THE NEW DISRUPTIVE MODELS

The new disruptors have introduced innovative business models that ensure convenience and value for the customers at affordable rates. They focus on building a healthy customer relationship as a way to gain loyalty. Here are some of the significant changes made by the new disruptors.

Co-creation of innovation: Facilitating customers through internet allows businesses to interact with their customers and form strong relationships directly.

D2C model: The Direct-to-Customer business model used by Warby Parker and Canva features mobile technologies that are more active and available to the customers with a 24/7 service. It allows customers to quickly reach out to the brands with any queries and issues, which builds their trust and loyalty.

Low-capital ecosystem models: D2C business models show how a disruptive startup can be formed with lower capital investments. Some of these models outsource their tasks developing an ecosystem where they share their infrastructure. They focus on testing, learning and adapting quickly.

THE THEORY OF DISRUPTION—WHAT STAYS THE SAME

No matter how hefty an investment business has or what great products it offers, disruptors' entry points will always be the same: the problem to solve and the job-to-be-done.

People might have the best products and services available to them, but they'll always complain about that one missing thing. That's something quite visible from the examples of Canva and Warby Parker. Canva found a way to aid people wanting to easily create beautiful graphics and designs at lower prices. Similarly, Warby Parker enabled people to have designer eyeglasses for less than $100.

TAKEAWAYS

According to Jeff Bezos, Amazon Founder, "customers are always beautifully, wonderfully dissatisfied." So, disruption takes the idea that customers are deprived of something they need, which is defined as job-to-be-done.

Disruption is the process whereby the new entrants gradually move from a corner to the center. They use technologies to enable the value chain, and employ new business models that deliver the new promise to customers and reduce entry barriers. Hence, they can progress at an exceptionally high speed, as seen with Canva and Warby Parker. Incumbents are in real danger, considering the power and speed of this new generation of disruptors.

New generation disruptors succeed by first identifying an unsolved customer problem and then conducting an in-depth analysis of ways to stream the value chain and redefine the business models using modern technologies that others haven't utilized effectively. The innovative use of technologies and unconventional strategies crushes the incumbents as new disruptors target their mainstream customers even quicker than ever.

Often incumbents try to avoid disruption and focus on sustaining what they already have. However, they fail to identify the job-to-be-done. To them, this wastes resources and time, and so they provide a straightforward way for new entrants to disrupt their businesses.

Hence, for incumbents to survive the deadly disruptors, they have to focus more on the industry's unattended sectors instead of flooding resources to create the digital versions of their analog selves, as we have seen in many sectors. In the next chapter, we will review some examples of incumbents that failed to handle disruptive innovation.

CHAPTER 13
LESSONS FROM COMPANIES THAT FAILED TO HANDLE DISRUPTION

"Learning and innovation go hand in hand. The arrogance of success is to think that what you did yesterday will be sufficient for tomorrow."
William Pollard, English clergyman

DURING A JOB INTERVIEW some years ago, on a beautiful Paris evening, I was going on and on about the peaks of my success during my career. The interviewer then threw me off with a surprising question: "So, tell me about your failures." For a moment, my impulsive brain wanted to answer that I have never had a failure, but then the truth came out in the form of the evident "any success story was preceded by a series of failures." The astonishment on his face was greater than the fresh evening air as he expected another answer, maybe.

Falling off a perch is not a pleasant feeling for an individual or a company. However, falling is a trait among warriors, and rising after a fall is a hobby for champions. For this to happen, an individual or a company needs to be sitting right up to the pile of all other competitors for several years to lose track and fall so hard that the company usually ends up in a bankruptcy file.

This chapter will look into six lessons we can learn from the downfall of companies that missed disruptive innovation. Each is explained by a real business history.

NOT HAVING A LARGER PERSPECTIVE

In 2004, a video rental company called Blockbuster owned 9,094 stores and employed approximately 84,300 people [162]. No one matched the size and magnitude of their video collection. When the world went from VHS to the shiny round discs, they survived.

In 2000, Blockbuster was approached by Netflix, a small company renting movies with a home delivery USP, with a price tag of $50 million [163]. However, Blockbuster thought that the new strategy was beneath them, and they felt they were far too big to be taken down, due to the number of stores/employees they had under their belt.

The same number of stores and employees became a liability when customers found it easier to rent a movie with a phone call, and later, just streaming any content. Blockbuster failed to see a market shift in consumer behavior right in front of their eyes, and eventually filed for bankruptcy in 2010.

Blockbuster was unable to switch its strategy, whereas Netflix went from home delivery to online streaming. By the end of 2020, Netflix had over 200 million users [26]. As of March 2021, it had grown a market value of $223.56 billion [27], continuing the impressive year-on-year growth enjoyed over the last decade.

NOT SWITCHING TO AN ALTERNATE PRODUCT

A company that manufactured photographic film, Kodak, blew the opportunity to step into the digital era because everyone thought it would reduce their physical film business. Their development team had developed the prototype of what was to be the first digital camera.

However, top management soon shot down the idea. They thought that if they started producing an alternative to their product, their original best-selling product would eventually fail. The management focused on selling the original core product, and Kodak missed out on being a digital industry pioneer.

Digital photography finally came in as a force and forced this champion company to file for bankruptcy in 2012 as they failed to launch a better alternative to their product [164].

HISTORY WILL NOT SAVE YOU

Toys-R-Us was a leading toy company in the '90s. It boasted of being the world's largest toy store chain, but got stuck with the internet boom in the 2000s. They contracted with Amazon to sell their toys online for ten years. However, Amazon's contract ended just four years after Amazon started exploring the world for other toy-making companies.

This was the ideal time for Toys-R-Us to go digital and jump into an e-commerce venture. Yet, past glory, just like Blockbuster, made them stagnant and persistent in their old business ways. They initiated an online program in May 2017. It was too late. Finally, they had to make a U-turn in September of the same year by filing for bankruptcy under the pressure of their $1 billion debt, and the robust online presence of other toy-making companies [1].

IGNORING USER EXPERIENCE EVOLUTION

Many companies became fatalities of the internet boom because they did not see the user being comfortable with the new technology in their own homes.

Borders Group, Inc. was an American book and music retailer. Borders did not expect customers to read and order most of their books online anytime in the near future. Simultaneously, Barnes & Noble and others like Amazon and Apple started selling paperback and e-versions online with a credit card's virtual swipe [165]. They jumped the game with their reading gadgets, which gave the user a book-like experience, while also owning several books in one device.

In the meanwhile, Borders grew its liabilities in the form of about 400 stores and more than 10,000 employees. They eventually filed for bankruptcy in 2011, 40 years after opening their first store in 1971. Barnes & Noble bought the reader database from Borders for a whopping $13.9 million [166].

OVERESTIMATING YOUR BRAND VALUE

This is one of the most discussed failures in consumer products' history, and is taught in many business schools.

Nokia, the technology giant, was the pioneer of cellular devices, and no other company came even close to its technological advancement and sales volume. However, they overestimated their brand value and did not see the paradigm shift. At this time, consumers experimented with a new kind of user interface, "the touch-screen" cellular device [167].

This company did not foresee a change in customer experience and stuck with its strategy using the old model. This decision was expected to save the customer from the current design and the level of difficulty if they changed too much.

What happened later and will keep happening in the future? Companies like Apple and others came out with a better user experience, thus revolutionizing the whole industry. Once Nokia decided to jump on the bandwagon, they were late and came up with software not liked by the users.

The result was that Nokia became an outdated cellular symbol which had once been the sign of prosperity and success. Overestimating your brand value can not only kill your present but your future as well.

IGNORING THAT SOCIAL IMPACT AND PURPOSE MATTERS

Nowadays, all companies are worried about their image because image can be tarnished worldwide with a single hashtag. In the early 2000s, this was not the case. This clothing tycoon learned this lesson the hard way.

Abercrombie & Fitch hit the gold mine when they rode pop culture and sold their articles of clothing to teens and young adults and became the talk of the town. However, their controversial employee statement, "we would rather burn clothes than give them to the poor," [168] began their downfall slide and pushed the brand popularity to an all-time low. Several hip brands boast the fast-paced culture—H&M, Forever21, and others added salt to the wound.

More than ever, purpose-driven innovation is an important driver in fostering innovative culture within organizations and a key differentiator.

TAKEAWAYS

Disruption implies moving and testing new ground and questioning a comfortable perch. As an innovator, one needs to learn from these misinterpretations to define your company's next path or venture. As described by the unsettled disruption framework, we must keep eyes open to external disruption trends and industry sensitivity.

You must find alternatives to strike the right balance so you can disrupt and thrive in innovation and business success. As an entrepreneur or intrapreneur, one needs to learn from the following misinterpretations:

1. Not having a broader perspective
2. Not switching to an alternate product
3. Understanding that history will not save you
4. Ignoring user experience evolution
5. Overestimating your brand value
6. Neglecting that social impact and purpose matter.

The next chapter will focus on the companies that flourished during the pandemic, and analyze how the unsettled disruption framework applies. Let's remember that disruptive innovation is never an overnight success and requires a systematic process that combines structural elements to make it happen.

CHAPTER 14
2020 DISRUPTORS

"There are two options: adapt or die."
Andy Grove

DISCUSSIONS ALWAYS HELP ME come up with better and clearer ideas. While talking to a friend, I recently learned about his company's struggles during the last two years trying to shift to the working-from-home culture before the pandemic. Regardless of the employees working remotely, the company wanted to make sure employees got the comfort, support, and technology they needed, which required a lot of work and investment. Despite several years of trying to onboard this change, the company failed to get the desired outcome because, beyond investment, they weren't convinced of the correctness of the move.

However, the pandemic forced them to go entirely virtual, and they did it within three weeks. How? By adapting to the new context and leveraging on emerging tools like Zoom video conferencing, and Slack business communication platform—this transformed the way they were working. But overall, it was the COVID-19 crisis that made the move happen and drove the belief that it was all possible.

During the past two decades, we witnessed how new entrants disrupt industry leaders within short periods. In relation, 2020 was a year of even faster disruption as it forced companies to adapt quicker than ever. It has once again confirmed Darwin's theory on humans' ability to adapt to the environment, not in thousands of years but in a few months.

This chapter will review some prominent cases of disruptive innovation and how these businesses flourished by helping to overcome the 2020 challenges.

TIKTOK—REAL PEOPLE, REAL VIDEOS

Do you use Facebook? I asked my sixteen-year-old cousin recently. And this member of Gen Z smiled at me and replied, "Of course not. Facebook is for older people. 'We' use TikTok."

Belonging to the '90s, I wasn't aware that the excitement of Facebook back in our day had now switched over to TikTok, the youngsters' new obsession in 2020. While confined in the four walls of the home and deprived of social interaction, not only teens but business professionals, political advocates, and even world leaders have found TikTok to be a great transitional tool.

Blake Chandlee, the Vice President of TikTok, during a conference in December 2020 [169], said, "You will get disrupted if you do not disrupt."

WHAT IS TIKTOK?

TikTok is the Chinese creative social media platform primarily driven by short-form video content. It launches challenges of various types to tap into the creativity of its users and generate engaging (if not addictive) content that is accessible via an infinite feed. With multiple niches from comedy, drama to horror, the app immediately caught fire among youngsters.

It was launched in September 2016 by a China-based company [170], ByteDance. In 2019, the app was downloaded about 738 million times [171], and the figure increased to over 2.6 billion by December 2020 [172].

As of September 2020, the app had over 850 million active users [173].

TikTok founder Zhang Yi Mien was a former Microsoft [174] software engineer and started his company in his twenties.

The following characteristics can sum up the application's highlights:

- This social media platform leverages the willingness of people to share their content.
- It combines compelling music tracks as the companion to the challenges set on the platform.
- It offers a set of creative filters and effects that can be applied to the videos.
- It is powered by AI algorithms that optimize content creation, curation, and recommendation.

STRATEGIC PURPOSE

TikTok's founder, Zhang Yi Mien, described the app's mission as combining the power of the internet with AI to revolutionize the way people obtain information. TikTok has become one of the quickest tech-based start-ups, and rivals industry leaders like YouTube, Netflix and Facebook [175].

The Chinese entrepreneurs such as Zhang showed how well they could achieve success in a freely competitive market internationally, beyond their own country where the internet is strictly regulated.

DISRUPTION TRENDS

TikTok leveraged three emerging trends to create opportunities. They are:

- The needs and expectations of demographic users: Gen Z cannot refrain from questioning the old ways of doing things and disrupting the status quo. The young environmentalist Greta Thunberg is one of the prime examples today. Moreover, Gen Zers are already a

substantial part of the active consumers worldwide, and their purchasing power will surely increase once they enter the workforce.
- The stay-at-home orders that helped drive TikTok's growth earlier in 2020 could spur additional user gains.
- Technology, mobile, and connectivity enable more people to access social networks combined with machine learning and artificial intelligence.

These trends form a strategic combo as Gen Z—the largest generation globally, making 32 percent of the total population [176]—is highly connected using mobile internet. Most TikTok users are young people who grew up with technology. They have a relatively short attention span and are more inspired by influencers than by ads. This generation has greater control over their lives than the ones before them.

TikTok aligned these consumer traits with the pandemic urgency to gain the spotlight. It came forward as an exciting way to keep people connected and standing together as a community during hard times.

INDUSTRY POWERS

Former social media platforms like Facebook are known for understanding their audience quite well. However, there is no denying that the ecosystem has changed and something was missing, giving birth to other platforms like Instagram and Snapchat.

Today, even these platforms are becoming old hat, while TikTok is the new talk of the town. This confirms that the social media industry is prompting new entrants as each generation is particular and has different ways to connect. To maintain market position, big platforms often compete with the existing rivals and fail to foresee the real threats that new entrants pose.

It's not about how Twitter overtook Vine or whether Reels will disrupt TikTok. Instead, it's more about how these companies understand the ecosystem and their consumers to identify the job-to-be-done, and then actively respond to the needs and demands for socializing while figuring out new ways to enter the industry.

JOB-TO-BE-DONE

Disruption is not a coincidence. We have witnessed disruptors before, and we can now identify some disruption patterns.

Gen Z demands unique and quick content, which existing social media platforms have failed to provide due to consolidating too many services and formats. They lost ground to TikTok, which came with a simple design to connect and engage. The revolutionary app enables everyone to be creative and encourages users to express their passion through their videos. However, there doesn't seem to be anything special about it, except the fact that TikTok's aim is really to tap into people's imaginations.

Whether it's for casual entertainment or formal education, Generation Z often prefers to consume content in rich video formats. While it's believed that young, digital-savvy audiences don't like being marketed to, this is not the case. Instead, Generation Z consists of online natives familiar with digital tactics and are also drawn to fresh content, such as original videos.

This is what makes TikTok videos and even ads so appealing. TikTok videos are typically characterized as raw, high-energy, and profoundly engaging. TikTok provides advanced yet simple-to-use tools for users or businesses to embed music and visual effects on videos. On TikTok, expressive Gen Z users tend to have significantly higher engagement rates than users on Instagram, Facebook, and Twitter.

VALUE CHAIN

TikTok simplified the value chain by leveraging on technology, providing a single-format platform, and offering in-app purchases. TikTok was released with a powerful video editing feature. At the beginning, it did not have to pay users with many views, giving them both innovation and low cost. It also allowed people to be more authentic, posting videos that show their funny or natural side, instead of encouraging editing to achieve a perfect look.

BUSINESS MODEL

As a macro business strategy, ByteDance has two versions of their TikTok app: one behind China's censored and closed-off internet, and the other for the rest of the world. Some analysts think that other Western companies should take note of this method.

TikTok's new business model is giving Instagram a tough time. Instagram leverages ad revenue, whereas TikTok depends upon in-app purchases while providing an ad-free feed. Thus, brands willing to advertise are only left with influencers.

In addition, users purchase coins to give to their favorite creators, exchanging the coins for digital gifts. User spending on TikTok is increasing even faster than user acquisition: as of April 2020, lifetime user spending totaled $456 million according to Sensor Tower [177].

As revealed by Bloomberg, the company made $2.5 billion in revenue in 2017 [178]. CB Insights estimated ByteDance as the most valuable Unicorn at $75 billion, which also surpassed Uber.

Another way TikTok leverages its model is that it signs a deal with music rights holders to give its users the consent to use 15-second music clips in their videos. These authorization arrangements are usually settled as a one-time fee for a particular library of tracks, or paid out on an ongoing royalty basis. Moreover, influencer culture is growing on TikTok, where influencers monetize the app, earning as much as $20,000 per branded video [179].

TECHNOLOGY

Imagine Facebook, YouTube, and Instagram all in one platform, driven by AI (Artificial Intelligence). Connie Chan [180], the venture partner at Andreessen Horowitz, discussed in a blog that ByteDance utilizes extreme

AI functions that are still new to the West. TikTok uses AI to sort videos to display to its users and learn about their tastes as they use the app. It is pretty different from other platforms like Facebook and Netflix that utilize AI to suggest posts rather than directly dictate their feeds.

The Artificial Intelligence [181] of the app dictates the users' interest: the more you use it, the more it learns what you like. In here, you can't select the content. There is a full-screen video that automatically starts playing. If you don't watch an entire video, the app will get your cue, and it will not recommend that kind of video again.

UNSETTLED

The onset of the global coronavirus pandemic and the associated lockdowns have further accelerated TikTok's trajectory. According to Sensor Tower, in the first quarter of last year alone, TikTok accumulated 315 million new downloads worldwide [182], a record-breaking quarter for an individual app.

As of spring 2020, ByteDance operates more than 20 apps in spaces ranging from news and video to music and mobile gaming [183]. Some, like TikTok, are international in scope. Others, like the news aggregator product Toutiao, have so far only been made available in China. According to CB Insights report [183], with each new product it launches, ByteDance leverages the same three key advantages it has cultivated in its core business areas, like news curation and short-form video:

- **Highly engaged young user base**: ByteDance is leveraging an audience of actively involved young people to facilitate growth.
- **Products engineered for virality**: With TikTok, ByteDance appears to have tapped into something powerful in the way that users currently want to engage with content. The top fifty content creators on TikTok have a following of more than the populations of Mexico, Canada, the UK, and Australia combined.
- **Personalization and recommendation algorithms**: One way to

think of ByteDance is not so much as a creator of content platforms but as an artificial intelligence laboratory specializing in developing algorithms that can match users with content, from video, music to news and e-commerce.

The rise of TikTok is not merely the story of a technology company's ongoing success. More importantly, it is about the emergence of the next generation of socially aware and digitally savvy users who abandon the habits and preferences of previous generations. As an evolution to social media, TikTok will soon become a disruptor of all the entertainment apps and websites, from YouTube to Facebook, Instagram, and Netflix.

However, at the bottom line, like other platforms, will TikTok be able to sustain its growth to the point of becoming the dominant creative social media?

ZOOM—ELEVATE EVERY ENCOUNTER

Zoom has now become a verb [184]. So, are you zooming today?

If I were to count the number of hours I spent on Zoom in the past eighteen months, it would definitely be more than 1,000 hours. Zoom is not confined to working professionals but is also used for virtual learning, gatherings, interviews, and many other things.

Compared to its 10 million daily meeting participants in December 2019, Zoom has grown considerably, with more than 300 million participants as of April 2020 [185]. In case you aren't familiar with Zoom, established in 2011, Zoom is a platform that is aimed at making "video communication frictionless" for everyone. It has leveraged the viral growth from its freemium model to use its direct sales force to identify the opportunity and channel those in B2B and enterprise accounts.

The company launched its software (Zoom) in 2013, which started to record profitability by 2019, and it was listed on NASDAQ-100 in April 2020 [186].

STRATEGIC PURPOSE

Delivering Happiness to Our Users is the motto of Eric Yuan, the founder of Zoom [187]. With this focus, Zoom keenly listens to its users and evolves accordingly. Mobility being users' key requirement today, video conferencing is just what they needed. Making this app user-friendly is Zoom's priority.

The Zoom platform fundamentally changes how people interact. The values of Zoom, including how it communicates, can be summarized in the following three points:

- Rich and reliable communication network
- Zoom meetings can be better than in-person meetings
- Promotes a way of thinking, working from home.

DISRUPTION TRENDS

The COVID-19 lockdown had a significant impact on business operations with a distributed workforce. It made virtual collaborations crucial for the survival of organizations, paving the way for Zoom to rise. On the top, travel restrictions made this even more evident, reducing not only tourism but business travels.

This pandemic has led millions of people to connect remotely through video conferencing apps for socializing, work, and going to school. Another fundamental trend is the infrastructure and technology that made this possible, including connectivity, bandwidth, and 4G and 5G.

INDUSTRY POWERS

Why did the industry leaders not respond to the situation sooner? That's because the incumbents overlooked the user experience and affordability of small and medium organizations. This created an opportunity for a new entrant with better services and lower prices. Cisco Webex, Google Meet,

Facebook Messenger, GoToMeeting, and Skype are Zoom's competitors. Skype and Webex, with their large cash stores, could certainly take control of the situation. But they did not see these segments as interested.

Zoom's success today has moved all the leading incumbents. As stated by CNN [188], "Facebook and Google are gunning for Zoom." Later, Facebook introduced Messenger Rooms, which allowed video conferencing with fifty people and no time limit. Google Meet became free and allowed users to host 100 participants without a time limit.

JOB-TO-BE-DONE

Beyond 2020 sanitary and social distancing measures, gone are the days when we used to travel for a one-hour meeting: now we Zoom. This saves time, energy, and money and clears away hindrances like distance, traveling time, and cost.

When Eric started Zoom, he was advised about the overloaded market condition and the associated risks. During those early days, Eric discovered that several small and medium companies were dissatisfied with the provided video collaboration tools. This helped him identify the job-to-be-done for small companies that included developing lower pricing, user-friendliness, no choppy videos, and easy to access via any device [189].

Consequently, Zoom could fulfill the user's needs so well that even technology leaders with incumbent licenses prefer to buy Zoom.

VALUE CHAIN

Zoom came up as a cost-effective model that suited individuals and small-scale organizations. It has connected the pieces that make purchasing considerably easier and thus ensure a good consumer experience. To further ensure easy purchasing, Zoom allowed monthly and annual subscriptions for users directly from its website, whereas the incumbents' offerings often required other products for effective use.

Zoom also recognized the need to integrate with other platforms with a close focus on consumer satisfaction and happiness. As a result, it came up with strategic integrations with YouTube Live, Otter.ai, and Slack. Zoom streamed the value chain to enable more comprehensive access to video conferencing services.

BUSINESS MODEL

The video conferencing solutions offered by the incumbents were expensive. Zoom, on the other hand, did not require any hardware and offered cheaper video collaboration. They started by offering a freemium model that benefited them by increasing their reach and ensuring that people would test their services.

A freemium business model is characterized by transforming free professional single accounts into enterprise accounts, once a great product experience lures them in. Zoom, designed on the freemium business model, ensures the service acts as a seamless entry point where salespeople and users can interact. It employs a highly specialized salesperson to build a strong relationship with the users from the other entry-point to bring the whole enterprise account onboard.

As of December 2020, its enterprise version costs start at $14.99 per month [190] and allows for unlimited meetings and minutes. It also offers a personal version for free and a custom enterprise version with a branded URL.

TECHNOLOGY

Zoom, being the true Cloud-based solution, does not require on-premises hardware. Its meeting connector software allows enterprises to deliver virtual meetings locally while using its public Cloud system to ensure scalability.

It also offers 3-in-1 Cloud meeting platforms that include HD video conferencing, web meetings, and mobility. The platform provides the facility of HD conferencing in gallery view, a full screen with the option to join through teleconferencing [191].

One of Zoom's goals is to make "true mobility." It means that mobile users should be free of limitations, unlike PC or laptop users [191]. To ensure that Zoom offered video sharing while conferencing to its mobile users, they could also join a link, create a meeting, and invite others. Recording meetings, conducting presentations, and annotating documents are some added features of the app.

UNSETTLED

Zoom aims to establish a reliable video communication platform that facilitates the work-from-home culture. Its broad consumer base, including individuals, businesses, and investors, makes phenomenal use of its freemium business model by capturing users and transforming them into paid subscribers after enjoying their free offering.

The success story of Zoom is inspirational. What started as an idea to tweak a former company's product succeeded in becoming an industry leader that's predicted to grow at a flourishing rate. Zoom, founded by Eric S. Yuan, is a prime example of how a company can reach the top of the heap even in today's era of hyper-competition.

SLACK—BE LESS BUSY

In this email-driven world, 3.8 billion email users exchange more than 306.4 billion emails each day in 2020 [192]. How could a new communication enterprise capture over one million daily active users in two years?

Slack is an internal communication platform that aims to revolutionize the way teams work. Slack has been a success from the beginning, with $1 billion valuations in 15 months. It is one of the fastest-growing companies ever [193].

Stewart Butterfield [194], a serial entrepreneur and the founder of Flickr, is the man behind Slack. In 2013, when Slack was launched, he witnessed dozens of companies instantly signing up. It seems like the timing was right.

STRATEGIC PURPOSE

Slack has come forth with the mission to make work more productive, pleasant, and simple through improved communication.

It has been observed how the existing solutions available to companies only add to frustration. That's exactly what the company wants to change by offering something that actually works.

Thus, the main challenge for Slack is to manage large groups within the enterprises. The company's value proposition arises from its willingness to cut down fragmentation in an organization's communication tools. One of its most significant elements is the ability to integrate with other tools and apps for information.

DISRUPTION TRENDS

For the past years, companies have been rethinking the way they work rather than returning to their old routines. With the lockdown and sanitary measures enforced by the COVID-19 pandemic, it became clear that we had been stuck in the 9-to-5 groove for too long and that it no longer served the organizations or the workers as it should. Thus, companies now need better means of communication to ensure smooth performance and more productivity, especially when employees are working remotely. [195]

Other disruption trends that helped Slack development are demographics, as new generations are looking for more flexibility and transparent communication. Digital transformation is also at the core of this evolution as most companies are looking to optimize different tools, like email, schedule, file-sharing, or Cloud storage, just to mention a few.

INDUSTRY POWERS

Slack has become a real substitute for several complex and fragmented solutions that were already well positioned as market leaders. Slack did not come with groundbreaking technology, but the industry was ready to be disrupted. Slack is not seen as an entire system but as an element used for different purposes like chatting, emailing, and file sharing, to strengthen each component rather than focusing on integrating them.

JOB-TO-BE-DONE

Slack creates value by offering an easy-to-use communication channel that is more enjoyable than emailing. For instance, it offers easy collaboration—people can connect to their team members from wherever they are. This answers the need to build team culture, ensure team support during remote working, improve efficiency, and much more.

Companies loved Slack for its affordable prices, smooth flow of information, and reduced workload. This helped Slack became one of the fastest-growing organizations with over 12 million active users in 2020, out of which 3 million are paid users [196].

VALUE CHAIN

Slack has made sure to align its operation and business models to guarantee a value proposition to its customers. It does so by offering a quality user experience that drives its customers to premium subscriptions. It can be seen as selling organizational transition. It had been extremely helpful during the pandemic by maintaining team cohesion and smooth communication flow. They streamed the teamwork value chain by integrating several fragmented functionalities such as messaging, emailing, file sharing, and team planning.

BUSINESS MODEL

Slack offers a freemium pricing model. Its free version is an excellent option for companies to try and check out if they want to utilize it in their business. It's easy to sign up and delivers great value.

Slack generates income mainly from paid subscriptions, which can be both monthly or annually. It is calculated based on the number of users the organization brings on Slack. The platform allows the users to archive data, which makes it even better for the companies. Considering its capability to deliver value, they prefer to try out the premium version not long after their trial.

TECHNOLOGY

Slack offers an exceptional user experience and is a good example of using existing technology to deliver value by combining both online and offline. Its technology makes the platform intuitive and easy to use for even someone who has never used technology before. It has an enormous customer support team located in different parts of the world to offer user assistance anytime. Thus, it quickly resolves its users' complaints and issues.

The software improves communication and integrates with other platforms like Dropbox, Google Drive, Twitter, etc. Slack drives information from all the integrated platforms to put them together in one place. It can even integrate across devices so that the users stay in touch all the time.

UNSETTLED

Slack's ability to align its value proposition, business, and operating model around making customers' lives simpler and more productive will solidify its place amongst breakthrough disruptors.

TAKEAWAYS

Disruptive innovation is a process and not an event. Zoom, TikTok, and Slack disruptive innovation stories unfolded in steps and continue to do so. This fact highlights the understanding that successful new entrants can identify the job-to-be-done, work out the incumbent's weak points, and deliver the right products or services.

Remember, technology itself is not disruptive. Instead, it helps disruption when utilized in the right way for the right job and at the right time.

Twenty twenty, the revolutionary year which changed the working and living conditions of people all over the globe, has been the right time for a lot of disruptors. The unorthodox situation created more jobs-to-be-done that some incumbents failed to recognize, paving the way for new entrants or emerging offers on the right path.

Business history is loaded with examples of disruptors taking over industries after entering with innovative and customer-oriented products and services.

You've just arrived at the end of the third part of this book; we have studied multiple disruptors such as Skype, Canva, Warby Parker, Starbucks and Airbnb, who captured their industries like wildfire. Microsoft and Disney are excellent examples of incumbents' self-disruption. We also find businesses failing to meet disruption, like Kodak, Toys-R-Us, Nokia, and Blockbuster, to close with some examples of 2020 disruptions, TikTok, Zoom and Slack.

At this point, you are ready to identify the multiple elements that make disruption happen, and to understand how companies faced and developed the disruption challenge. I hope that you use this unsettled disruption framework as a source of inspiration to define your next innovation journey.

However, before ending, in the fourth part of this book, we will close with the driver of this journey, "your strategic purpose," and remind us that this is the best time to innovate by embracing purpose-driven disruption.

PART IV
THE FUTURE

CHAPTER 15:
HOW PURPOSE CAN HARNESS DISRUPTION

"We are all living together on a single planet, which is threatened by our own actions. And if you don't have some kind of global cooperation, nationalism is just not on the right level to tackle the problems, whether it's climate change or whether it's technological disruption."
Yuval Noah Harari

IN THE 18TH CENTURY, the transportation industry's incumbents—railway and horse carriages—tried to hold off the automobile's advancement. From 1865 to 1896, for more than thirty years, anybody who owned a car had to hire a man to walk ahead with a red flag to alert the possible danger to passersby [197].

Most recently, the same story happens. The leading automobile manufacturers wasted millions of dollars to inhibit such transportation revolutions as the electric car and other innovations. They could not prepare themselves to face reality and were draining their resources to suppress the inevitable. As new entrants such as Tesla come into play, disruption trends such as climate change and regulations have changed the landscape, and other car manufacturers started the transition. Some reacted quickly and invested heavily in their transformation, and others were left behind. Still, we will see the future of mobility to be more than electric cars.

This is a clear depiction of how sustainability is driving disruptive innovation. It makes businesses ponder over actual tweaks that they can perform to enhance value and quality for the customers. Thereby, it gives them a direction in which to move, reducing friction and increasing convenience not only for their customers but also for the whole ecosystem.

However, like automobile manufacturers at one time, several incumbents fail to recognize this future. They focus on securing their existing revenue, leaving sustainability and customer value aside. Consequently, they leave a gap for others to fill, which serves as an entry point for disruption. Hence, for a business to flourish in the long run, sustainability is the key.

Purpose provides a "north star" for employees to rally around. It is a framework for decision-making and a way to connect personal values to personal and professional success. As management guru Gary Hamel puts it: "Remarkable contributions are typically spawned by a passionate commitment to transcendent values such as beauty, truth, wisdom, justice, charity, fidelity, joy, courage and honor [198]."

At the same time, companies with purpose are better able to motivate employees and satisfy customers, so it is not surprising that these companies also have higher business success. In *Corporate Culture And Performance* [199], Harvard Business School professors John Kotter and James Heskett show that purposeful, value-driven companies outperform their counterparts in stock price by a factor of twelve over a decade-long period.

SUSTAINABILITY—THE ULTIMATE PURPOSE OF DISRUPTION

In a recent article in Digital Initiative at *Harvard Business Review* [200], Rebecca Henderson talked about climate change's global issue and how we, together, need to act upon it instantly. She urged businesses to use their resources, especially technology, strategically, and contribute to combating environmental change through their platforms. She rightly said, "The world is on fire, and we have very little time to control it. If we fail to do so, the aftermath will be dreadful and irrevocable."

Most industry leaders are having a hard time dealing with disruption.

They face denial, unwillingness to give up on the "business as usual," and concentrating their focus and resources on short-term goals.

It appears these incumbents see pollution and climate issues as something that will eventually disappear one day. But we don't have fairies in this real world to solve our problems; we need to address them on our own. Many business owners cannot accept that the world is evolving and that the future will not be the same as it is today. Instead, they believe in eternal business as usual and predict the future based upon past experiences. They think their success agents will remain the same despite a drastic shift in technology, consumer behavior, operational policies, and regulations.

A well-known example of denial is organizations' inability to switch to renewable energy sources instead of continuing to drain the limited resources. Some companies in sectors such as plastic packaging, food, and fashion are denial cases, making them significantly vulnerable to disruption.

REASONS FOR COMPANIES' INEFFECTIVE RESPONSE TO CHANGES

Companies' failure to respond to changes effectively is primarily due to the hectic routines that keep them hooked to daily affairs with not enough time to work on the changes. They also do not give it due importance. These companies are usually under tremendous pressure to rake in their target income, so that embracing transformation, requiring space and deep restructuring, looks trivial.

Moreover, it is challenging for them to put aside their years-long hard work to achieve expertise in what they do, which leads them to denial.

But that's not the complete picture; several big brands like H&M, Unilever, and IKEA are adopting self-disruption to make the long due transformation. They are reframing their processes and moving towards sustainable business models to develop relevance in the future.

PURPOSE-DRIVEN INNOVATIVE DISRUPTION

Regardless of how devastating the crisis we witness is, it is also a wake-up call for a change—mostly an advancement. Now it's up to us whether we take this opportunity and improve, or stay where we are. The COVID-19 pandemic has forced the world towards advancement. Businesses that abide by it are progressing despite the imposed restrictions. In contrast, those who decided to stick to their traditional operations, paying no heed to the survival requisites, have met their fate: shut down.

In straightforward terms, for businesses to stay in the market, they have to adopt an in-depth transformation, including disruptive innovation. Although that alone is not enough, that's one of the basic requirements of the current time. Moreover, self-disruption and innovation, which once gave a competitive edge, need to be sustainable and integrated into the whole changing system.

In the prevailing situation, organizations of all sizes and types focus on restructuring and reinventing their business. Such a self-disruptive approach has enabled them to find unsolved problems and new opportunities to answer jobs-to-be-done. Going further, detailed observations of recent disruptions have revealed a shift in disruptive practices to being purpose-oriented. This new lever of change has been the most effective and sustainable of all the other approaches.

Let's dive into the workings of this major lever of the unsettled disruption framework as the driver for disruptive innovation, the strategic purpose.

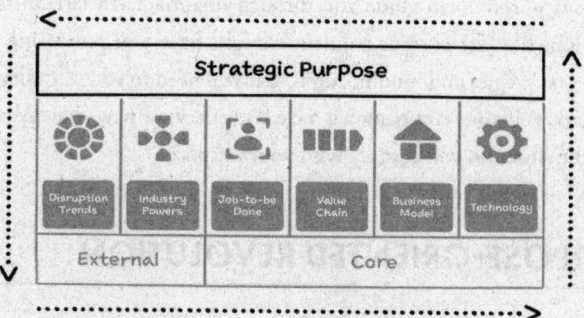

Figure 19 - Unsettled Disruption - Strategic Purpose

PURPOSE SHOWS A STRONG ENTRY POINT FOR DISRUPTION

A triggering factor pushing businesses into adopting a disruptive framework can be the purpose that gives meaning to their existence.

Sometimes, entrepreneurs or small startups focus on short-term gains, directing all their resources without recognizing the more significant issues which offer a heavier and more sustainable return. They get so engrossed in shallow purposes that they miss out on the more meaningful rewards. Fortunately, the emergence of social innovation and new purpose-driven startups are changing this trend.

You may be wondering how to identify these rewarding opportunities and acknowledge your purpose. For that, you need to ask yourself the following questions:

- Why did you establish the business?
- Why do you strive to be different from your competitors?
- What are your customers more concerned about?
- How can your offering bring a purposeful social, economic, or environmental change and impact?

Your purpose can guide you through unanticipated circumstances. Situations like the current pandemic might have you pondering upon the new strategies and modifications that you need to adapt to survive in the market. If your company has a clear north, your new strategy to deal with the situation will comply with your purpose.

PURPOSE-ORIENTED REVOLUTION

The world of disruption is undergoing a major revolution. This parallel disruptive force is based on emerging values and norms circulating throughout the commercial world. Not only customers but also investors and even employees are also focusing on associating with organizations that endeavor to create a positive social impact.

According to the IBM Institute for Business Value, in 2020 more than 40 percent of consumers consider a business's social impact when making purchasing decisions [201]. Brands like Warby Parker, Patagonia, Tala, Seventh Generation, and Ben & Jerry's have shown ways to maintain and win even loyal consumers.

Let's learn from their stories of purpose-oriented approaches to the disruption that became a part of their brand identity.

SEVENTH GENERATION

In the present-day scenarios, consumers seek to support businesses that offer valuable products and services while ensuring a positive social influence. Keeping this in mind, Seventh Generation, the largest cleaning equipment supplier in the US, has evolved as an eco-friendly entity committed to offering sustainability and human health. This has rewarded the brand with accelerated growth, large purchases, customer goodwill, and earned media [202].

The brand's mission is to change consumer behavior to maintain sustainable health for generations to come. One of its primary goals is to deploy 100 percent renewable energy sources by 2025. It further plans to provide zero-waste packaging and improve organizational diversity.

PATAGONIA

Studies have shown that 62 percent of global consumers aspire to associate with companies that take action on social issues [203]. Patagonia, an American clothing company, makes an excellent example of such an approach. The brand has been an active advocate of environmental campaigns for a long time. Patagonia has changed its mission from a product-environment hybrid to a solely environment-friendly entity; they reflect their engagement in all their communication strategy and initiatives [204].

BEN & JERRY'S

Ben & Jerry's aims at providing a lot more than just ice creams. The brand is dedicated to promoting social justice and creating awareness of environmental issues. Ben & Jerry's mission approaches include partnering with NGOs and other social and environmental activists. To derive impactful results, the brand connects with professionals in the relevant field [205].

WARBY PARKER

Warby Parker was mainly started with the mission to promote people's right to see clearly. This mission enabled the eyewear brand to become a major disruptor of the industry as it came up with an affordable pair of glasses that most people could afford. Moreover, they donate a pair of glasses for every purchase made with them. It didn't take the company long to be valued at over $1 billion.

TALA

Tala is a microfinance company offering credit to small businesses. The brand was formed with the worldwide mission to make short loans to businesses and individuals with lower credit scores or who lacked financial identities. It provides quick loans as small as $40—in about 60 seconds.

In regions like Southeast Asia and Africa, there are few people with a credit score. Instead of considering the person's financial situation, Tala considers several thousand data points on a borrower's mobile phone: merchant transactions, web searches, social media, etc. It analyzes the credibility of a person based on these points.

The brand operates to form a strong and sustainable relationship with global consumers who return to them as often as they need extra cash for their business. Tala has lent over $1 billion to more than 4 million customers in Kenya, the Philippines, and Mexico [206].

SUSTAINABILITY, THE DRIVING FORCE BEHIND FUTURE DISRUPTIVE INNOVATION

Disruptive innovation has been drastically changing societies over time. We have upgraded from horse-drawn plows to steam engines and even smartphones. These innovations have immensely improved our lives in unimaginable ways, and they continue to do so.

Nowadays, the world faces major social and environmental issues, including water and air pollution, scarcity of resources and climate change, among many others. In the present time, it is crucial to be part of the movement to develop sustainable products and services that can last longer without impacting the environment. One of the currently observed driving forces behind disruptive innovation is sustainability.

EMPOWERING CONSUMERS TO BECOME MORE SUSTAINABLE

Companies attempting to rule disruption through sustainability have already started offering products and services that enable business sustainability.

Beyond the examples discussed in this chapter, we see more companies moving in the same direction. For example, since 2007 Marks and Spencer has offered garments that are washable at temperatures lower than 30°C [207], which reduces energy bills. Unilever offers another example by providing concentrated detergents that require less water than traditional ones.

Some of you may think that is not enough, and it is not. But we must start somewhere and find the birth point of many industries to this purpose-driven movement.

UN PROMOTES INNOVATIVE DISRUPTION TO MAKE THIS WORLD A BETTER PLACE

Surprisingly, crisis brings us closer to our surroundings and strengthens our ties of cooperation and solidarity in a way that perhaps was never experienced before.

According to the World Economic Forum, the pandemic may cost the world economy over $1 trillion (optimistic loss) or $82 trillion in a worst-case scenario [208]. This devastating situation has already crippled many economies and hasn't even stopped yet. If conditions were to remain the same, it would lead to unprecedented catastrophes.

To combine the need for more innovation and sustainability priorities, we can take the UN's 17 Sustainable Development Goals (SDGs) blueprint to transform our world. These goals are a direction to restoring the economy working towards a sustainable future. Through this guideline, the UN has highlighted the need for businesses and communities to join hands and take collective actions towards making this world a better place.

GOAL 1: No Poverty
GOAL 2: Zero Hunger
GOAL 3: Good Health and Well-being
GOAL 4: Quality Education
GOAL 5: Gender Equality
GOAL 6: Clean Water and Sanitation
GOAL 7: Affordable and Clean Energy
GOAL 8: Decent Work and Economic Growth
GOAL 9: Industry, Innovation and Infrastructure
GOAL 10: Reduced Inequality
GOAL 11: Sustainable Cities and Communities
GOAL 12: Responsible Consumption and Production
GOAL 13: Climate Action
GOAL 14: Life Below Water
GOAL 15: Life on Land
GOAL 16: Peace and Justice Strong Institutions
GOAL 17: Partnerships to Achieve the Goal

These development goals, also referred to as Global Goals, were given out in 2015 to fight poverty and ensure equality on earth by 2030 [209]. In the form of sustainable goals, the UN has given us an extensive list of jobs-to-be-done, thus promoting disruptive innovation. Since these goals are integrated, the steps taken towards the fulfillment of one will affect the others. However, their ultimate objective is to achieve social, environmental, and economic sustainability.

2020 CHANGED PARADIGMS

Drastically changing the paradigms, 2020 has made it possible for companies to realign their status and redefine their purpose in a very short time. The good news is that the transformation is not always as difficult or costly as assumed, as most of the time impacts are considered short- and mid-term. All one has to do is look beyond the present situations and devise a strategic purpose.

Many firms are already looking into leading-edge opportunities that can generate massive profits in the long run while addressing major world problems. Business leaders are keenly moving towards social and environmental causes. They are looking for ways to actively respond to climate changes through transforming cities, production, supply chain, systems—food, transport, energy, to mention a few.

We can highlight some examples in the fashion industry. This sector is calling out for disruptive innovation to design and produce clothes of higher quality. It is essential to shift from the perception of clothing as a disposable item to a durable product. The industry needs to adapt to consumer demands and evolution. Numerous people regularly like to wear new clothes; others do not favor donning an article more than a few times as it gets worn out and shabby. On the other hand, a pair of jeans or T-shirt that lasts in quality and design, they wouldn't have a substantial reason to discard it.

To understand how disruption can work, below are a few practical examples to take inspiration from. Disruptive rental models designed a compelling value proposition, particularly if we consider changing customer needs. As of now, we have started to see examples of specialized garments such as MUD Jeans that offer high-quality denim, a subscription for babywear by Vigga, and Rent the Runway, which targets working women and offers an "unlimited" subscription service.

VIGGA is a Danish clothing brand offering kids and maternity wear. Following a circular design, their product-service model allows users to lease organic children and maternity clothes, saving them time and money while benefiting the system and the manufacturer.

The problem to solve is that kids-wear is mainly the clothing industry section that creates excessive waste, as the children quickly outgrow the clothes. Unfortunately, less than half of the total useless clothing items are collected for recycling, and only 1 percent of them are recycled.

As a solution to frequent baby clothing purchases, Vigga offers a subscription-based service, allowing parents to lease baby clothes. The first package is delivered a few days before the birth of the baby. When the baby grows out of those clothes, another package arrives with larger clothes, and the parents return the first package to the company.

VIGGA's leasing model can reduce kids-wear waste by 80 percent. It forwards the outgrown clothes to new users and collaborates with the clothing recycling company that uses garments to produce newer ones.

Through this disruptive approach, VIGGA contributes to reducing the need to purchase new clothes and allows parents to save money. According to VIGGA, parents can save $2100 during the first parenting year by subscribing to this model [210].

These examples reframed all traditional sectors by redefining the jobs-to-be-done, restructuring the value chain, proposing a new business model, and leveraging technology to deliver their offer.

TAKEAWAYS

Sitting and worrying about the present or joining leaders in creating a sustainable future—the choice is yours. Leveraging an untapped market through transformation opens doors to unimaginable growth and profitability, making this the best time to innovate.

As learned from the examples of Warby Parker, Tala, Ben & Jerry's and Patagonia, disruption based on solid purpose is more powerful and sustainable than others. These companies question the current state of offerings in the industry. They identify the sectors that haven't been answered yet. Hence, they use their business platforms to solve far more significant problems than just selling a pair of glasses or ice creams.

These days, customers are much more passionate about the business that offers benefits like helping people in need or protecting animals and the environment. Hence, when setting your purpose for disruption, make sure to add lasting social or environmental benefits to it.

Once a business has its purpose, all of its decisions align with it to collectively achieve the final goal. It also forces enterprises to try different technologies and investigate methods to shape these technologies' use following their purpose. For this reason, we left the strategic purpose at the end of the book to remind us that it is the central source of inspiration and cornerstone for your unsettled disruption journey.

CHAPTER 16
THE ROAD TO UNSETTLED DISRUPTION, GIVEN DAVID AND GOLIATH

"Everything is possible. The impossible just takes longer."
Dan Brown

EVERYTHING IS POSSIBLE—THIS is the lesson I was led into at the age of nine, after reading David and Goliath for the first time.

Here's a brief of the story [211]. Goliath was the giant of the Philistines. He was the champion who challenged the Israeli fighters to wrestle him and decide the country's fate in a single encounter instead of the constant war. None other than David dared to step ahead and face the forbidding giant. Regarding Goliath the giant's fighting skills and full-armed support, David remained undismayed.

What's even more interesting is that David only brought a sling and a stone-filled pouch, against the giant's inexorable sword and elephantine shield. Goliath was the first one to charge in the field. At that moment, David located an unshielded spot in the giant's armor and with all the power he had threw a stone at it. That extremely accurate shot to the head was enough to knock Goliath out, giving David a clear path to victory. David marched in and won the war.

THE DISRUPTION LESSON

These past few years, we have seen many Davids emerge and disrupt several industries, defeating their Goliath with strategic and unconventional approaches that the giants didn't see coming. These disruptors created value for the consumers by identifying the jobs-to-be-done, redefining the value chain, restructuring the business model—all of this through leveraging on technology one way or the other.

EVERYTHING IS POSSIBLE

Relating the stories of unsettled disruption, we have seen how everything is indeed possible. Keeping the same hope alive, we need to believe that we can achieve our goals no matter how powerful the opponents are. If you have a short time to act, work on creating striking energy that meets your goals quickly. The development and release of vaccines within a compressed period of time in 2020 seems to be a good example, or consider the plans to go to Mars in 2025. Even if many still are not sure about the vaccine's efficacy or skeptical of that well-renowned trip, their agility and speed beat the rest. If they fail, it is an opportunity to learn what not to do.

Picturing Goliath at first might be overwhelming because of his enormity, expertise, skills and weapon. But none of that could stand against David's strategic approach, which easily knocked the giant out despite David's small stature. If David had chosen to throw the stones all over the place randomly in a rapid-fire, spotting the giant's weak point would not have been possible. Therefore, he took his time and position to pinpoint the right spot to target. One precise shot proved to be much more advantageous than emptying the entire pouch without a purpose.

Understanding disruption through the systematic unsettled disruption framework can help you to connect the dots and devise an effective disruption strategy. Remember what David did: he focused on precision.

Creating a focus and directing it to achieve accuracy is essential to a successful disruption. This enables a better understanding of your purpose and properly redefining the opportunities based on it.

In Goliath and David's story, the rule was simple: one champion had to confront Goliath in a one-time fight, and the winner would rule the land. Although David was no match to Goliath's strength, the giant did not stand a second chance, nor could any other fighter continue the fight.

Despite that, David's smart approach quickly made him the winner. This shows how important it is to believe in yourself and in the future. When talking about the future, it is essential to understand that it largely depends upon your actions today. The way you handle it changes everything.

For a successful future, you need to plan systematically and keep your pace high enough to meet your goals tomorrow.

HUMAN EVOLUTION—WHAT WILL HAPPEN IN 30 YEARS?

What we do today will come back to us later. The choices, decisions, strategies, and channels we use to meet our ends today will determine their usage, availability, and effectiveness in the future. That's how we write human history, which unfolds over time, giving us a throwback of what we have done and how we reached where we are today.

I firmly believe in our capabilities to create a sustainable yet viable future. Although we often feel despair, staying optimistic and strictly focusing your eyes on the target can help you ignite unimaginable creativity and innovation, thus leading you to join the community of successful disruptors worldwide. One of the most prominent innovations these days is companies' incorporation of societal needs into their corporate objectives.

TAKEAWAY

Purpose-Driven Disruption—No More an Exception but a Rule. Considering the significance of a sustainable future, finding the right way to achieve it is the next big question.

How to upgrade the status of purpose-driven disruption from an exception to a rule?

It is not easy to channel the existing corporate world's disruption potential and redesign the economy to attain sustainability with over 7 billion people worldwide. This makes bridging today's reality with tomorrow's opportunity "the elephant in the room." [212]

The current enormity of social and environmental changes with The UN's Seventeen Sustainable Development Goals [213] as the backdrop has encouraged several big organizations to significantly contribute to a positive environment. So far, collaborative, inclusive, circular, and de-carbonized business models are emerging business approaches adopted by most businesses for a sustainable economy.

The impact of human activities on the earth has been quite significant in the past few decades. Scientists have identified it as a new geological era called the Anthropocene—the era in which human activities have set a new life course for all the systems alive [214].

For a disruptor, no company is irreplaceable, and no business model is safe from disruption. There are so many Davids around, and many of them are still in the making. There are massive opportunities for rebuilding the economy for a prosperous and sustainable world. The world is on the edge of the Disruptive and Sustainability Revolution.

CONNECTING THE *UNSETTLED DISRUPTION* DOTS

JOSE BOWEN'S TED TALK, "Beethoven as Bill Gates," [215] describes the history of music from ancient times to the eighteenth century when we had only a handful of performers, which also included a selected class of experts who were available to play costly instruments. To hear music at the time was nothing short of a privilege; you had to go to a concert. In other words, if you wanted to enjoy the works of stalwart musicians such as Bach or Mozart, you had to travel to Germany.

At the time, the piano was the only musical instrument that could be mass-produced. It is a perfect example of innovation at its best, as most of the other apparatus were very expensive. Hence, the piano enabled more people to play music. However, the significant disruption came with Gutenberg's introduction that made it possible to print and distribute music at another level.

Beethoven figured out how to connect these "disruption dots." He leveraged these new disruptive trends to shake an industry that served only a niche market focusing on a privileged group. The realization that he didn't need to travel to have people listen to his music changed the music industry forever. Beethoven used technology to print and sell his music to others, who would then play his music for maximum reach.

Beethoven identified a job-to-be-done to bring music to the masses. He changed the way music was distributed. This was an entire revamping of the value chain that now offered a more accessible way of listening to music. He established an innovative business model by selling his music and getting royalties, compared to being paid only for a live performance. He leveraged technology, the piano, and the printing press to achieve his goal of bringing music to a bigger public. Beethoven beat seasoned musicians like Mozart and Bach by harnessing the power of disruptive innovation.

LESSONS FROM 2020

Let's wrap up. We started this book by asking how so many companies couldn't see disruption coming while others harness the power of disruptive innovation.

In the last chapters, we saw how several companies flourished by building new models and answering to the changing customers' needs and challenges of our world today. Back in 1995, did you believe that you would never take pictures on film/paper again, rent a house for holidays from a stranger, create your awesome social media posts in a few clicks or perform customer meetings via video conference services?

Many organizations have become irrelevant as they fail to adjust to the shifting trends and disrupt themselves. Companies such as Kodak, Blockbuster, and Tower Records have seen their businesses diminish over the years. What happened to them will happen to many other companies as the pace of the "exponential revolution" is more significant than the radical changes several industries are facing.

The year 2020 has been a wake-up call for many and, at the same time, the best time to innovate. Still, some were lost in their traditional ways, or lacked the imagination to turn around and start over. They focused too much on the present and fear to evolve for the future, ignoring the major trends. These disruption trends are shaping the new world: technology, climate change, new generations, new consumer expectations are accelerating this move and challenging most traditional industries. Let's mention a few examples of these trends to explore the dimension of the multiple opportunities.

ARTIFICIAL INTELLIGENCE BEYOND A BUZZWORD

Artificial Intelligence (AI) is not just a buzzword anymore but is changing our daily lives exponentially. The rise of computing power has made this change possible as better computers are at hand to handle vast swathes of data. This data, along with Artificial Intelligence, helps computers diagnose illnesses (IBM's Watson program [216]), recognizes faces (Facebook's pattern recognition [217]), and so on.

ENABLING SMART TRAVELING BY THE AUTOMOTIVE INDUSTRY

Autonomous Cars will be a thing of reality soon enough [218]. Meanwhile, the auto industry faces severe disruption as most people don't need to own a car these days. You can simply order a car to show up at your location, using your smartphone. Noisy streets and roads will be replaced by electric cars, which produce negligible noise.

CHANGES IN THE WAY WE LIVE IMPACT THE REAL ESTATE INDUSTRY

Real Estate prices will also see a change as 2020 has shown us that working remotely is a distinct possibility. People can move further away from busy business districts and afford to live in the suburbs or countryside. Commutes will be shorter and sporadic and thus lead to ease in traffic congestion.

FOCUSING ON GREEN ENERGY TO POWER UP THE WORLD

Electricity generation will also be cleaner and more affordable as solar and wind energy will dominate electricity generation in the next few decades [219]. Low-cost electricity translates to an abundant supply of clean as well as potable water. The supply of clean drinking water is a real challenge these days, especially in third-world countries. With its provision, ample availability of clean water will solve a lot of sanitary and disease-related problems.

BLENDING MACHINERY WITH THE AGRICULTURE INDUSTRY

The agriculture industry will see considerable changes as more machinery comes into play [220]. Manual labor will be negligible, and even meat products could be produced in labs. This will lead to more affordability of food items and thus leads to food security for all. Cattle rearing requires a lot of space, and if these food products can be produced in a lab, a lot of agricultural lands will be free to be utilized for other purposes.

CONSIDERATION OF HEALTH CONSCIOUSNESS IN THE FOOD INDUSTRY

As digital health care becomes a reality, more people will realize the benefits of activity and leading a healthy life. Food choices will become better as different apps and plans advise us on what to eat and what not to.

For the other side, as the world population keeps increasing, food demand will also increase, as reported by CSIRO, Australia. A rough estimate shows such demand to increase by 14 percent per decade [221]. How will the scarce resources of our world feed 10 billion people in 2050 at this rate?

These innovations pose a new question [222]. One such question is whether you can consume burgers, flour, or snacks made of insects. Meat production hurts the climate, and we may see a shift towards meat-free food intake. Another possible breakthrough may be algae farming. This has the potential to maintain biodiversity while meeting consumer needs.

MIGRATING ONLINE AND ENVIRONMENTAL SENSITIVITY IN THE FASHION INDUSTRY

The fashion industry may see similar change trends as customer demand and industry tend to shift towards more sustainable and eco-friendly production models [223]. This industry causes much waste, and brands are looking to change this as customers demand more "greener" products. COVID-19 has pushed this sector to embrace the online marketplace. Previously, brands used to churn out many collections per year, but this trend may change due to sustainability demands.

SHIFTING FROM PAPER TO ELECTRONIC CURRENCY

Bitcoin has taken the world by storm in the financial world as its value increases day by day. This shows that the market is ready to move towards a tech-centric currency.

HOSTING CLASSES REMOTELY IN THE EDUCATION INDUSTRY

The education field has also been affected by COVID-19 as academic discourse moves to the online world. The proliferation of smartphones has increased the chances of students in remote places getting a world-class education. Online platforms such as Khan Academy [224] host a world of resources for anyone who wants to learn, be it students or everyday people.

AN EYE INTO THE FUTURE

We can expect that many of the incredible changes will take longer to impact than is currently believed. But more challenges are coming, and their effects will be major. We need to be ready to embark on taking these changes in our stride to create a better future. It is time to gather all the innovators and entrepreneurs to solve the upcoming challenges that face humankind.

It is clear that disruption does not happen overnight; major changes mature with time and become powerful enough to disrupt an industry. *Unsettled Disruption* provides you with a step-by-step framework to understand disruption thoroughly so that you can put in place a plan to find and define your strategy.

UNDERSTANDING DISRUPTIVE INNOVATION AND WINNING OVER IT

Entrepreneurs are often the ones who develop new products or services to revolutionize an entire industry. They start small in a niche market and then scale the product to appeal to a broader group of people. They need not be intimidated by bigger players because established companies are probably not interested in developing these low-margin products at first.

The term "disruptive innovation" might confuse or scare companies; hence, they need to understand its definition. It is not always necessary for an innovation to be disruptive. However, disruption is always about innovation.

Therefore, businesses must learn how to unsettle disruption and identify new opportunities to define their strategy. The idea of a disruption process can raise many questions regarding how to tackle such a strategy shift. The best strategy to answer these questions is, to begin with, a systematic process like unsettled disruption that enables you to recognize all internal and external elements and then frame the opportunities.

Let's recall the framework levels—external, the core, and the strategic purpose.

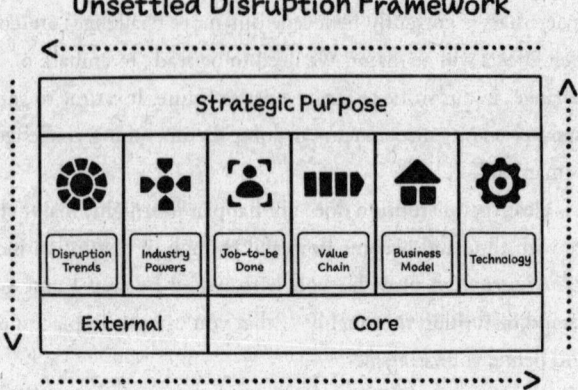

Figure 20 – The Unsettled Disruption Framework

EXTERNAL

Predicting the future is no easy task. Experience tells us that we need to monitor what is happening outside our comfort zone. It would help if you start by looking into external disruption trends to help you connect the dots and get a complete understanding of how they may affect your business. Many companies are affected by the top executives failing to see the change coming. Their systems only monitor and measure known risks and uncertainties.

According to Porter's Forces analysis, disruption is likely to occur in industries where the threat of new entrants and substitutes is more significant. In such situations, disruptors can find ways to overcome entry barriers and offer better alternatives.

Even if the entry barriers are high, balance in the remaining forces often offers sufficient support to disruptors. Disruptors search for ways to shift powers among the buyers and suppliers, leverage environmental trends and regulations, and then combine opportunities with value chain, business model innovation, and technology. Therefore, you can predict the chances of disruptive innovation in your industry using Porter's Five Forces framework—by assessing your position, risks, and opportunities. These two elements disruption trends and industry powers compose the External level of the unsettled disruption framework.

UNSETTLED DISRUPTION CORE

At this level, you must consider four core elements—jobs-to-be-done definition, value change analysis, business novel innovation, and specify how to leverage on technology to deliver your value.

In Jobs-to-be-done, companies usually look at data to predict customer behaviors but ultimately fail due to the non-recognition of jobs-to-be-done. We must empathize with the customer to understand the fundamental drivers to define the "jobs-to-be-done." JTBD explains how people do not just buy stuff for the sake of it; instead, they buy for a specific purpose or, more precisely, to do a "job." By linking this necessity with our strategy, you can home in on a world of innovative possibilities as disruption is driven by customers.

Value chain analysis helps innovators look beyond standard means of efficiency and look for ideas to disrupt the status quo. This breakdown leads to an overall identification of how disruption occurs in a market, or how to disrupt one's very own value chain. Shortening the value chain has already disrupted existing powerhouses in their respective industries. Such industries include PC manufacturers, retail furniture, hospitality, and tech-related sectors. Several sectors that are now seeing the full potential of technological advancements in their fields will be vulnerable in the future. These include industries with long or complex value chains and high costs relative to the value of technology-driven disruptions.

Business model innovation represents the high-level architectural plan for your disruptive innovation. It describes your innovative product or service, its market, and the economic engine that will enable you to meet your profitability and growth objectives.

Now is the time to learn from the leading examples of business models. In the embryonic phase of a project, we start by testing various business models and learning approaches; hence, it is sometimes called trial and error. This process of discovery has an element of uncertainty and risk. Only after successful trials can you scale up and expand.

Technology. When planning to disrupt, businesses need to know that technology can only aid in disruption, and it is not the sole prerequisite to achieve such a disruption. Companies often invest a large chunk of their resources into finding ways to use technology without looking into the problems they want to solve.

We can start by observing whether technology can disrupt or help you disrupt your target market. Understanding this will help us identify ways to use technology to deliver value to the customers.

PURPOSE-DRIVEN DISRUPTION

The unsettled disruption framework is based on a well-defined purpose. You must question the current state of offerings in your industry and identify any loopholes or sectors that are not delivering your purpose. Once a business has its purpose, all of its decisions align with it to collectively achieve the final goal. It also forces enterprises to try different technologies and investigate various methods to achieve that goal.

Disruptive innovation is here to stay. Through this book, you have explored not just the tools but also several examples of incumbents who came out stronger; and new entrants in a new disruptors generation—some who missed the mark, and others that flourished in 2020.

These examples are a source of inspiration to help you connect the dots with your idea, project or business. The sooner we connect the dots on how to embrace unsettled disruption, the sooner you can make progress as an innovator. Using the forces of disruption for our collective good, innovators and entrepreneurs can provide an immense service to humankind. The journey towards disruption is paved with trials and tribulations, but these are important in self-discovery for any individual, community, or business entity. Disruption has the power to shape our future, and we must align our goals to achieve change.

ONE MORE THING

First, thank you for reading *Unsettled Disruption*. To help you through the process of unsettled disruption, I have created a set of resources that will be available on my website (jncnova.com), which include:

- Download a free *Unsettled Disruption* workbook, a step-by-step guide, and templates to develop your disruptive innovation project.
- Subscribe to my monthly newsletter featuring best practices, case studies, and news.
- Join a community of purpose-driven disruptors on their journey.

PS.
The gift of feedback is always deeply appreciated. Can you do me a small favor?

Please visit the site where you purchased this book, Amazon or any other site, and share a review. It would be extremely valuable to me. Thank You.

ACKNOWLEDGMENTS

WRITING THIS BOOK HAS been one of the most rewarding and inspiring journeys of my career. The seeds of *Unsettled Disruption* come from everyone who ever taught me lessons and worked with me over the past twenty-five years. For that, there are many people to thank: mentors, mentees, colleagues, team members, entrepreneurs, and innovators who inspired every chapter of this book and helped me weave together the stories and structure for this framework.

As with all the great projects I have experienced, this has resulted from a team effort. This book is not an exception. Every chapter has been possible thanks to the fantastic contribution of others. It took me more than one year to create the first version, but it took me years to understand disruption, and in these times of "Exponential Revolution," our learning will still evolve.

As I write my dedication, I realize that I owe much to my family and closest friends, as they have given me the support and confidence to write this book. My son provides me with renewed inspiration and drive every day. My husband supports every step of this journey by giving me his trust and love.

Special thanks to my dear friends Nora, Clotilde, Marylene, Marta, and Catalina, who cheered me on through every step of the journey and encouraged me to make this book happen. Thank you to my dear friend Claus who is always there when I need advice and a rational German perspective.

Since my first experience in the construction sector and then into fast-moving consumer goods, financial services, telecom, banking, retail, and other industries, all of these experiences helped me polish this work entitled *Unsettled Disruption*. The mentors who crossed my path during the past twenty-five years of my career are endless—most of them are still my friends. I would like to thank all of you for allowing me to create an amazing, innovative journey since my first internship twenty-five years ago in Colombia through my experiences across several countries as an innovator and my most recent entrepreneurial effort. Thank you, Milton Ascensio, Juan Camilo Peña, David Ballestas, Jean Philippe Ruault, Jean-Francois Schreiber and Muriele Rouyer.

A huge thank you to more than 300 mentees, entrepreneurs, and intrapreneurs who inspired me to write this book as we worked together to unsettle markets and find new opportunities, many of which became the foundation of this book.

Thank you to the most influential business and disruption thinkers: Clayton Christensen and his fantastic work, which led my first steps on to the disruptive innovation path; and Michael Porter, who for years has been providing us the frameworks to understand business complexities better. Both were the inspiration for many chapters in this book.

Thank you to Stanford GSB professors Stefanos A. Zenios and Haim Mendelson, who, through their Design for Disruption and Business Models Analysis and Design lectures and experiences, helped me refine this book's ideas even more.

Thank you to Chantal, an innovator, founder, and my first reader. She provided early feedback on the entire manuscript and reassured me about the relevance of this book and the opportunity to help others.

I cannot end this acknowledgment without thanks to my publisher,

Koehler Books, and the awesome team who saw the opportunity to help readers with their disruption journey and apply the concepts and framework to real life, regardless of their business expertise. Thank you for trusting me as a new author and helping me to share my experience with you.

Finally, to you, "my reader"—the reason I sat down to write this book. Thank you for trusting me. I hope this book brings you a new vision. Remember that anything is possible; we just need some help to take the first step. I want to leverage your creativity and power. Please use this book to create a path to transform the future. Thank You.

ABOUT THE AUTHOR

JUANA-CATALINA IS A SERIAL Intrapreneur and Entrepreneur. On her twenty-eighth birthday, she immigrated from Colombia to the United States, living and working in several countries since that time, currently living in the South of France.

For the past two decades, Innovation & Disruption have been strong suits of Juana-Catalina's, creating value and developing new offers.

She has worked in several industries, which provided her expertise. The list includes fast-moving consumer goods, financial services, mobile retail, cloud storage, digital identities, digital transformation, and social innovation across Asia-Pacific, Europe, Latin America, and North America.

She is also a start-up advisor, mentor, and author, and the founder of *JnC Nova*. This company helps startups, intrapreneurs, and other innovators accelerate their development and grow their businesses by streamlining their disruptive innovation processes.

Juana-Catalina is a consultant and executive coach for the Stanford

GSB Seed-Stanford Institute for Innovation in Developing Economies and Stanford GSB LEAD programs for global executives and entrepreneurs.

She is also a mother, a citizen, a social activist, and the founder of *beterre*, an early-stage startup with the mission to raise awareness of plastic pollution and share simple ways to reduce plastic waste.

Juana-Catalina holds a Bachelor in Engineering, M.S in Marketing, MBA, and has a corporate innovation certificate from Stanford's LEAD program.

REFERENCES

[1] M. Corkery, "Toys-R-Us Bankruptcy," *The New York Times*, 19 September 2017. [Online]. Available: https://www.nytimes.com/2017/09/19/business/dealbook/toys-r-us-bankruptcy.html.

[2] Airbnb, "A Message from Co-Founder and CEO Brian Chesky," 5 May 2020. [Online]. Available: https://news.airbnb.com/a-message-from-co-founder-and-ceo-brian-chesky/.

[3] J. Kelly, "Two Major Airlines Have Announced Massive Layoffs," *Forbes*, 26 August 2020. [Online]. Available: https://www.forbes.com/sites/jackkelly/2020/08/26/two-major-airlines-have-announced-massive-layoffs/?sh=5b48f0e3235f.

[4] McKinsey & Company, "McKinsey Global Innovation Survey," McKinsey & Company, 2020. [Online]. Available: https://www.mckinsey.com/business-functions/strategy-and-corporate-finance/how-we-help-clients/growth-and-innovation.

[5] "Entrepreneurs: How To Define Your World's Future In The Exponential Age," *Forbes*, 19 April 2017. [Online]. Available: https://www.forbes.com/sites/rodnturner/2017/04/19/entrepreneurs-how-to-define-your-future-in-the-exponential-age/?sh=19888fba474f.

[6] CNBC, "Zoom walks back claims it has 300 million daily active users," CNBC, 20 April 2020. [Online]. Available: https://www.cnbc.com/2020/04/30/zoom-walks-back-claims-it-has-300-million-daily-active-users.html.

[7] Ycharts, "Zoom is Now Worth More Than the World's 7 Biggest Airlines," Ycharts, 15 May 2020. [Online]. Available: https://www.visualcapitalist.com/zoom-boom-biggest-airlines/.

[8]   UNESCO, "1.3 billion learners are still affected by school or university closures, as educational institutions start reopening around the world, says UNESCO," UNESCO, 29 April 2020. [Online]. Available: https://en.unesco.org/news/13-billion-learners-are-still-affected-school-university-closures-educational-institutions.

[9]   M. Sheetz, "Elon Musk is 'highly confident' SpaceX will land humans on Mars by 2026," CNBC, 1 December 2020. [Online]. Available: https://www.cnbc.com/2020/12/01/elon-musk-highly-confident-spacex-will-land-humans-on-mars-by-2026.html.

[10]   "Web Summit 2020," Lisbon, 2020.

[11]   "Oxford Reference," Oxford University Press, 2021. [Online]. Available: https://www.oxfordreference.com/view/10.1093/oi/authority.20110803100000653.

[12]   C. Christensen, "Disruptive Innovation," 2020. [Online]. Available: https://claytonchristensen.com/key-concepts/.

[13]   C. Christensen, "Biography Clayton Christensen," n.d. [Online]. Available: https://claytonchristensen.com/.

[14]   M. E. R. R. M. Clayton M. Christensen, "What Is Disruptive Innovation?" Harvard Business Review Magazine, December 2015. [Online]. Available: https://hbr.org/2015/12/what-is-disruptive-innovation.

[15]   T. Taulli, "Are Most Of Your Product's Features... Useless?" *Forbes*, 24 February 2019. [Online]. Available: https://www.forbes.com/sites/tomtaulli/2019/02/24/are-most-of-your-products-features-useless/?sh=1462b9ed4459.

[16]   B. Zhang, "These are the 10 most useless features in cars," *Business Insider*, 13 May 2019. [Online]. Available: https://www.businessinsider.com/cars-worst-features-2019-5?IR=T.

[17]   C. Karmin, "Marriott to Take On Airbnb in Booming Home-Rental Market," *The Wall Street Journal,* 29 April 2019. [Online]. Available: https://www.wsj.com/articles/marriott-to-take-on-airbnb-in-booming-home-rental-market-11556535600.

[18]   Dollar Shave Club, "Dollar Shave Club," 2020. [Online]. Available: https://www.dollarshaveclub.com/.

[19]   Online retail consultancy Slice Intelligence, "Online Razor Market," 2015. [Online]. Available: https://www.rakutenintelligence.com/.

[20]   B. Booth, "What happens when a business built on simplicity gets complicated? Dollar Shave Club's founder Michael Dubin found out," CNBC, 24 March 2019. [Online]. Available: https://www.cnbc.com/2019/03/23/dollar-shaves-dubin-admits-a-business-built-on-simplicity-can-get-complicated.html.

[21]   The New York Times, "Dollar Shave Club Sells to Unilever for $1 Billion," 20 July 2016. [Online]. Available: https://www.nytimes.com/2016/07/20/business/dealbook/unilever-dollar-shave-club.html?_r=0&auth=login-google.

[22]   "Dollar Shave Club," [Online]. Available: https://www.dollarshaveclub.com/.

[23]   Dollar Shave Club, "DollarShaveClub.com—Our Blades Are F***ing Great," 6 March 2012. [Online]. Available: https://www.youtube.com/watch?v=ZUG9qYTJMsI.

[24]   Northumbria University, "The Design Thinking Tricks That Netflix Use to Keep Us Watching," Northumbria University, n.d. [Online]. Available: https://www.northumbria.ac.uk/study-at-northumbria/courses/ma-design-management-distance-learning-dtdpdz6/design-thinking-tricks-netflix/.

[25]   Macrotrends, "Netflix Revenue 2006-2020 | NFLX," 2021. [Online]. Available: https://www.macrotrends.net/stocks/charts/NFLX/netflix/revenue.

[26] J. Alexander, "Netflix surpasses 200 million subscribers, but has more competition than ever in 2021," The Verge, 19 January 2021. [Online]. Available: https://www.theverge.com/2021/1/19/22238877/netflix-200-million-subscribers-q4-earnings-bridgerton-emily-paris-cobra-kai-queens-gambit.

[27] "Market capitalization of Netflix (NFLX)," Market Cap, March 2021. [Online]. Available: https://companiesmarketcap.com/netflix/marketcap/#:~:text=As%20of%20February%202021%20Netflix,cap%20according%20to%20our%20data..

[28] M. Zetlin, "Blockbuster Could Have Bought Netflix for $50 Million, but the CEO Thought It Was a Joke," Inc., ND. [Online]. Available: https://www.inc.com/minda-zetlin/netflix-blockbuster-meeting-marc-randolph-reed-hastings-john-antioco.html.

[29] J. Alexander, "The entire world is streaming more than ever—and it's straining the internet," The Verge, 27 March 2020. [Online]. Available: https://www.theverge.com/2020/3/27/21195358/streaming-netflix-disney-hbo-now-youtube-twitch-amazon-prime-video-coronavirus-broadband-network.

[30] S. Godin, "What Dave just did," 16 June 2008. [Online]. Available: https://seths.blog/2008/06/what-dave-just/.

[31] R. Branson, "Turning challenges into opportunities," Virgin, 28 February 2020. [Online]. Available: https://virgin.fr/branson-family/richard-branson-blog/turning-challenges-opportunities.

[32] J. Siddiqui, "Understanding the History of Disruptions in Retailing," 14 February 2017. [Online]. Available: https://jawwad.me/understanding-history-disruptions-retailing/.

[33] D. Bailey, "Why Airbnb Is Disruptive Innovation and Uber Is Not," INC, 27 April 2017. [Online]. Available: https://www.inc.com/dave-bailey/why-airbnb-is-disruptive-innovation-and-uber-is-not.html#:~:text=Airbnb%20is%20the%20classic%20example%20of%20a%20disruptive%20product&text=A%20low%2Dcost%20solution%20to,stay%20at%20a%20nice%20hotel..

[34] D. Gerdeman, "The Airbnb Effect: Cheaper Rooms For Travelers, Less Revenue For Hotels," *Forbes*, 27 February 2018. [Online]. Available: https://www.forbes.com/sites/hbsworkingknowledge/2018/02/27/the-airbnb-effect-cheaper-rooms-for-travelers-less-revenue-for-hotels/?sh=526b465ed672.

[35] C. R. Melissa Swift, "Long Live the Walkman," KORN FERRY, n.d. [Online]. Available: https://www.kornferry.com/insights/articles/walkman-leadership-disruption.

[36] Apple , "Let's Talk iPhone event '11," San Francisco, 2011.

[37] T. Worstall, "The Economic Importance Of Disruptive Innovation," *Forbes*, 14 January 2016. [Online]. Available: https://www.forbes.com/sites/timworstall/2016/01/14/the-economic-importance-of-disruptive-innovation/?sh=4f1dad7a7111.

[38] United Nations Population Fund, "Menstruation and human rights—Frequently asked questions," United Nations Population Fund, May 2020. [Online]. Available: https://www.unfpa.org/menstruationfaq#Menstruation%20cannot%20be%20managed%20properly.

[39] M. E. Porter, Competitive Strategy: Techniques for Analyzing Industries and Competitors, Free Press, 1998.

[40] K. D. T. H. ,. D. S. D. Clayton M. Christensen, Competing Against Luck: The Story of Innovation and Customer Choice, *Harper Business*, 2016.

[41] M. E. Porter, Competitive Advantage, S & S International, 2004.

[42] S. D. Anthony, "Kodak's Downfall Wasn't About Technology," *Harvard Business Review*, 15 July 2016. [Online]. Available: https://hbr.org/2016/07/kodaks-downfall-wasnt-about-technology.

[43] PESTLE ANALYSIS, "What is PESTLE Analysis? An Important Business Analysis Tool," 2020. [Online]. Available: https://pestleanalysis.com/what-is-pestle-analysis/.

[44] Future Today Institute, "Amy Webb," 2021. [Online]. Available: https://futuretodayinstitute.com/amy-webb/.

[45] A. Webb, "The 11 Sources of Disruption Every Company Must Monitor," *MIT Sloan Management Review*, 10 March 2020.

[46] Pestle Analysis, "Social Factors Affecting Business," 25 February 2015. [Online]. Available: https://pestleanalysis.com/social-factors-affecting-business/.

[47] "How Well-off is China's Middle Class?," China Power, n.d. [Online]. Available: https://chinapower.csis.org/china-middle-class/.

[48] The World Bank Org., "The many faces of the learning crisis," The World Bank Org., [Online]. Available: https://openknowledge.worldbank.org/bitstream/handle/10986/28340/9781464810961_Ch03.pdf.

[49] B. L. Megan Beck, "Three Signals Your Industry Is About to Be Disrupted," 11 June 2016.

[50] M. E. Porter, "How Competitive Forces Shape Strategy," *Harvard Business Review*, March 1979.

[51] Plastemart, Leading Packaging Companies in 250 Billion USD Plastics Packaging Market. http://www.plastemart.com/plastic-technical-articles/global-plastics-packaging-market-leading-manufacturers/2400

[52] G. Wearden, "More plastic than fish in the sea by 2050, says Ellen MacArthur," *The Guardian*, 19 January 2016. [Online]. Available: https://www.theguardian.com/business/2016/jan/19/more-plastic-than-fish-in-the-sea-by-2050-warns-ellen-macarthur.

[53] R. Harrabin, "UN commits to stop ocean plastic waste," BBC News, 5 December 2017. [Online]. Available: https://www.bbc.com/news/science-environment-42239895.

[54] Frost & Sullivan, "New Product Development Issues and Challenges," Frost & Sullivan, 2020. [Online]. Available: https://ww2.frost.com/growth-opportunities/new-product-development/.

[55] C. Christensen, "Jobs to be done," Christensen Institute, 2020. [Online]. Available: https://www.christenseninstitute.org/jobs-to-be-done/.

[56] M. Greenwald, "Nielsen BASES Breakthrough Innovation List For 2019 Announced Today," *Forbes*, 3 December 2019. [Online]. Available: https://www.forbes.com/sites/michellegreenwald/2019/12/03/nielsen-bases-breakthrough-innovation-list-for-2019-announced-today/?sh=4bd8a5f963fb.

[57] "Easter egg," The Culture Wiki, [Online]. Available: https://culture.fandom.com/wiki/Easter_egg.

[58] "Hunt for the origins of the Easter Egg," [Online]. Available: https://www.maturetimes.co.uk/hunt-origins-easter-egg/.

[59] "The story of Ferrero Group," Ferrero, n.d.. [Online]. Available: https://www.ferrero.com/the-ferrero-group/a-family-story.

[60] "Kinder Surprise," Wikipedia, [Online]. Available: https://en.wikipedia.org/wiki/Kinder_Surprise#:~:text=The%20Italian%20company%20Ferrero%20began,eggs%20have%20been%20sold%20worldwide..

[61] H. Roberts, "Inside Italy's real life 'Willy Wonka' chocolate factory: How world's richest chocolatier invented Ferrero Rocher, Nutella, Kinder and hid secret recipes in Arabic in Cairo to keep them from spies," *Daily Mail*, 15 November 2015. [Online]. Available: https://www.dailymail.co.uk/news/article-3311559/The-real-life-Willy-Wonka-world-s-richest-chocolatier-invented-Ferrero-Rocher-Nutella-Kinder-hid-secret-recipes-Arabic-Cairo-away-spies.html.

[62] Starbucks, "Starbucks Company Profile," [Online]. Available: https://www.starbucks.com/about-us/company-information/starbucks-company-profile.

[63] Starbucks, "Starbucks Reports Q4 Fiscal 2020 Results," 29 October 2020. [Online]. Available: https://investor.starbucks.com/press-releases/financial-releases/press-release-details/2020/Starbucks-Reports-Q4-Fiscal-2020-Results/default.aspx.

[64] S. Mohammed, "Nine 'Design-Thinking' Tips For Growing A Successful Business," 10 October 2018. [Online].

[65] L. B. Foster, "5 Ways Starbucks is Innovating the Customer Experience," *QSR Magazine*, May 2018. [Online]. Available: https://www.qsrmagazine.com/consumer-trends/5-ways-starbucks-innovating-customer-experience.

[66] Starbucks, "Executive Team," [Online]. Available: https://stories.starbucks.com/leadership/kevin-johnson/.

[67] H. Schultz, *Onward: How Starbucks Fought for Its Life without Losing Its Soul*, Rodale Books, 2012.

[68] E. H. Schein, Organizational Culture and Leadership (The Jossey-Bass Business & Management Series) Paperback, John Wiley & Sons, 2010.

[69] Starbucks, "Starbucks Company Timeline," [Online]. Available: https://www.starbucks.com/about-us/company-information/starbucks-company-timeline.

[70] I. C. Campbell, "Starbucks says nearly a quarter of all US retail orders are placed from a phone," The Verge, 30 October 2020. [Online]. Available: https://www.theverge.com/2020/10/30/21540908/starbucks-app-q4-earnings-mobile-payments.

[71] S. P. V. E. I. S. J. V. L. Scott D. Anthony, "2018 Corporate Longevity Forecast: Creative Destruction is Accelerating," INNOSIGHT, 2018.

[72] A. Klement, When Coffee and Kale Compete, CreateSpace Independent Publishing Platform, 2018.

[73] C. Darwin, *On the Origin of Species*, 1859.

[74] A. Sulleyman, "Netflix's biggest competition is sleep, says CEO Reed Hastings," *Independent*, 19 April 2017. [Online]. Available: https://www.independent.co.uk/life-style/gadgets-and-tech/news/netflix-downloads-sleep-biggest-competition-video-streaming-ceo-reed-hastings-amazon-prime-sky-go-now-tv-a7690561.html.

[75] Wikipedia, "Pony Express," Wikipedia, 10 December 2020. [Online]. Available: https://en.wikipedia.org/wiki/Pony_Express.

[76] Online Highways, "Western Union," Online Highways, 2020. [Online]. Available: https://www.u-s-history.com/pages/h1801.html.

[77] Macrotrends LLC, "Facebook Market Cap 2009-2020 | FB," Macrotrends LLC, 20 December 2020. [Online]. Available: https://www.macrotrends.net/stocks/charts/FB/facebook/market-cap.

[78] Statista, "Twitter: quarterly revenue 2011-2020," Statista, 2 November 2020. [Online]. Available: https://www.statista.com/statistics/274568/quarterly-revenue-of-twitter/.

[79] J. Topolsky, "The End of Twitter," *The New Yorker*, 29 January 2016.

[80] Statista, "Number of monthly active Twitter users worldwide from 1st quarter 2010 to 1st quarter 2019," Statista, 14 August 2019. [Online]. Available: https://www.statista.com/statistics/282087/number-of-monthly-active-twitter-users/.

[81] D. Z. Morris, "Today's Cars Are Parked 95% of the Time," *Yahoo Finance*, 13 March 2016 . [Online]. Available: https://finance.yahoo.com/news/today-cars-parked-95-time-210616765.html.

[82] BlaBlaCar, "About us," BlaBlaCar, n.d.. [Online]. Available: https://blog.blablacar.fr/about-us.

[83] Harvard Business School, Institute for Strategy & Competitiveness, "The Value Chain," Harvard Business School - Institute for Strategy & Competitiveness, [Online]. Available: https://www.isc.hbs.edu/strategy/business-strategy/Pages/the-value-chain.aspx.

[84] Stefanos Zenios, "Design for Disruption," Stanford Graduate School of Business, 2019. [Online]. Available: https://www.gsb.stanford.edu/exec-ed/programs/stanford-lead/curriculum/courses/design-disruption.

[85] IKEA, "About the IKEA group," IKEA, 2019. [Online]. Available: https://www.ikea.com/ms/en_JP/about_ikea/the_ikea_way/our_business_idea/a_better_everyday_life.html.

[86] Warby Parker, "History," n.d.. [Online]. Available: https://www.warbyparker.com/.

[87] Kiva, "Kiva," Kiva, 2021. [Online]. Available: https://www.kiva.org/.

[88] LYFT, "Lyft," Lyft, 2020. [Online]. Available: https://www.lyft.com/.

[89] MARS, "Case Study Dell Distribution and Supply Chain Innovation," MARS, 2021. [Online]. Available: https://learn.marsdd.com/article/case-study-dell-distribution-and-supply-chain-innovation/.

[90] J. Magretta, "The Power of Virtual Integration: An Interview with Dell Computer's Michael Dell," *Harvard Business Review*, 1998.

[91] DELL Direct Case Study - GRADUATE SCHOOL OF BUSINESS Stanford University, 2000.

[92] Statista, "Dell's market share of PC unit shipments 2011-2020, by quarter," Statista, 20 October 2020. [Online]. Available: https://www.statista.com/statistics/298976/pc-shipments-worldwide-dell-market-share/.

[93] P. Bajpai, "Analyzing Starbucks' Value Chain," Investopedia, 21 October 2020. [Online]. Available: https://www.investopedia.com/articles/investing/103114/starbucks-example-value-chain-model.asp.

[94] KNOEMA, "Number of Starbucks Stores Globally, 1992-2020," 25 June 2020. [Online]. Available: https://knoema.com/infographics/kchdsge/number-of-starbucks-stores-globally-1992-2020.

[95] Starbucks Corporation, "Form 10-Q—For the Quarterly Period Ended March 29, 2020," Starbucks Corporation, 2020.

[96] Airbnb, "About us," September 2020. [Online]. Available: https://news.airbnb.com/about-us/.

[97] IKEA Invades America - *Harvard Business Review*, 2004.

[98] Statista, "IKEA's number of stores worldwide from 2013 to 2020," Statista, 30 November 2020. [Online]. Available: https://www.statista.com/statistics/1060053/number-of-ikea-stores-worldwide/#:~:text=Number%20of%20stores%20of%20the%20IKEA%20Group%20worldwide%20from%202013%20to%202020&text=As%20of%20the%20end%20of,of%20445%20IKEA%20stores%20worldwide..

[99] Statista, "Annual revenue of the IKEA Group worldwide from 2001 to 2020," Statista, November 30 2020. [Online]. Available: https://www.statista.com/statistics/264433/annual-sales-of-ikea-worldwide/.

[100] C. Anderson, *Free: The Future of a Radical Price*, Hachette Books, 2009.

[101] "Haim Mendelson," 2020. [Online]. Available: https://www.gsb.stanford.edu/faculty-research/faculty/haim-mendelson#:~:text=Haim%20Mendelson%20is%20the%20Kleiner,at%20the%20University%20of%20Rochester..

[102] Haim Mendelson, "Business Model Analysis and Design," Stanford Graduate School of Business, 2019. [Online]. Available: https://www.gsb.stanford.edu/exec-ed/programs/stanford-lead/curriculum/courses/business-model-analysis-design.

[103] C. Cakebread, "Amazon launched 22 years ago this week—here's what shopping on Amazon was like back in 1995," Insider, 20 July 2017. [Online]. Available: https://www.businessinsider.com/amazon-opened-22-years-ago-see-the-business-evolve-2017-7?IR=T.

[104] T. Wolverton, "Auctions getting lost in Amazon's jungle," CNET, 31 July 2001. [Online]. Available: https://www.cnet.com/news/auctions-getting-lost-in-amazons-jungle/.

[105] Amazon, "Amazon Marketplace a Winner for Customers, Sellers and Industry—New Service Grows over 200 Percent in First Four Months," 19 March 2001. [Online]. Available: https://press.aboutamazon.com/news-releases/news-release-details/amazon-marketplace-winner-customers-sellers-and-industry.

[106] I. Gonzalez, "Atari Founder Predicts 'Massive Benefit,' Disruption in Tech Future," 10 November 2017. [Online]. Available: https://sanantonioreport.org/atari-founder-predicts-massive-benefit-disruption-in-tech-future/.

[107] D. Granderson, "Mars Inc.'s Acquisition of VCA: More Fidos, Fewer Sugars," Packaged Facts, 12 January 2017. [Online]. Available: https://www.packagedfacts.com/Content/Blog/2017/01/12/Mars-Incs-Acquisition-of-VCA-More-Fidos-Fewer-Sugars.

[108] R. Casadesus-Masanell, "Hilti Fleet Management (A): Turning a Successful Business Model on Its Head," CASE HBS CASE COLLECTION, MAY 2017 2017. [Online]. Available: https://www.hbs.edu/faculty/Pages/item.aspx?num=52550.

[109] O. G. a. R. Sauer, "Hilti Fleet Management (A): Turning a Successful Business Model on Its Head," HARVARD Business Publishing, 2017. [Online]. Available: https://www.ccmp.fr/collection-harvard-business-publishing/cas-hilti-fleet-management-a-turning-a-successful-business-model-on-its-head.

[110] Y. P. A. S. F. E. Alexander Osterwalder, The Invincible Company How to Constantly Reinvent Your Organization with Inspiration From the World's Best Business Models, 2020.

[111] Jim Marous, "Easy Banking: The Simple Strategy," The Financial Brand, n.d.. [Online]. Available: https://thefinancialbrand.com/26881/simple-easy-banking-strategy-jm/.

[112] *Quote 2010 by publisher Tim O'Reilly.*, 2010.

[113] Twitter Inc, "Twitter Announces Fourth Quarter and Fiscal Year 2020 Results," Twitter Inc., 9 February 2021. [Online]. Available: https://www.prnewswire.com/news-releases/twitter-announces-fourth-quarter-and-fiscal-year-2020-results-301225278.html#:~:text=2020%20revenue%20was%20%243.72%20billion,of%207%25%20year%20over%20year..

[114] "Twitter, Inc. - 10K Form," Twitter Inc, 2020. [Online]. Available: https://d18rn0p25nwr6d.cloudfront.net/CIK-0001418091/6074f5a7-baba-42c7-8f28-31accf8f3e8e.pdf.

[115] Spotify Technology S.A., "Spotify Technology S.A. Announces Financial Results for Fourth Quarter 2020," Spotify Technology S.A., 2 March 2021. [Online]. Available: https://investors.spotify.com/financials/press-release-details/2021/Spotify-Technology-S.A.-Announces-Financial-Results-for-Fourth-Quarter-2020/default.aspx.

[116]   R. Ord, "Peloton Moving Toward Subscription Model, Says CEO," 12 September 2020. [Online]. Available: https://www.webpronews.com/peloton-subscription-model/.

[117]   Unilever, "Unilever acquires Dollar Shave Club," Unilever, 20 July 2016. [Online]. Available: https://www.unilever.com/news/press-releases/2016/unilever-acquires-dollar-shave-club.html.

[118]   Macrotrends, "Alibaba Revenue 2011-2020 | BABA," Macrotrends, [Online]. Available: https://www.macrotrends.net/stocks/charts/BABA/alibaba/revenue.

[119]   Alibaba Group Holding Limited, "Alibaba Group Announces March Quarter and Full Fiscal Year 2020 Results," Alibaba Group Holding Limited, 22 May 2020. [Online]. Available: https://www.businesswire.com/news/home/20200522005178/en/Alibaba-Group-Announces-March-Quarter-and-Full-Fiscal-Year-2020-Results#:~:text=In%20the%20fiscal%20year%20ended,180%20million%20consumers%20outside%20China..

[120]   Airbnb, "About us," Airbnb, [Online]. Available: https://news.airbnb.com/about-us/.

[121]   S. R. Johnna Montgomeriea, "Owning the consumer—Getting to the core of the Apple business model," *Accounting Forum,* pp. 290-299, December 2013.

[122]   I. Luck, "How Tesla Used A $0 Marketing Strategy To Dominate A Market," Marketing Strategy, 5 September 2019. [Online]. Available: https://www.marketingstrategy.com/marketing-strategy-studies/how-tesla-used-a-0-marketing-strategy-to-dominate-a-market/.

[123]   "Market capitalization of Tesla (TSLA)," Companies Market cap, March 2021. [Online]. Available: https://companiesmarketcap.com/tesla/marketcap/.

[124] M. R. M. S. Ulrich Pidun, "How Do You "Design" a Business Ecosystem?," BCG, 20 February 2020 . [Online]. Available: https://www.bcg.com/publications/2020/how-do-you-design-a-business-ecosystem.

[125] Wikipedia, "Wikipedia:Wikipedians," Wikipedia, 2021. [Online]. Available: https://en.wikipedia.org/wiki/Wikipedia:Wikipedians#:~:text=The%20English%20Wikipedia%20currently%20has,contributors%20participate%20in%20community%20discussions..

[126] Wikipedia, "Wikimedia Foundation," Wikipedia Foundation, 2021. [Online]. Available: https://en.wikipedia.org/wiki/Wikimedia_Foundation.

[127] OECD, "Financial Markets, Insurance and Pensions—Digitalisation and Finance," 2018. [Online]. Available: http://www.oecd.org/finance/Financial-markets-insurance-pensions-digitalisation-and-finance.pdf.

[128] eBay, "eBay Company," [Online]. Available: https://www.ebayinc.com/company/.

[129] M. Kane, "eBay picks up PayPal for $1.5 billion," CNET, 18 August 2002. [Online]. Available: https://www.cnet.com/news/ebay-picks-up-paypal-for-1-5-billion/.

[130] B. A. O. N. B. Rao, "Fusion of Disruptive Technologies: Lessons from the Skype Case," Pergamon, 2006.

[131] F. Lardinois, "Microsoft Teams is coming to consumers—but Skype is here to stay," Techcrunch, 30 March 2020. [Online]. Available: https://techcrunch.com/2020/03/30/microsoft-teams-is-coming-to-consumers-but-skype-is-here-to-stay/.

[132] J. Cauz, "Encyclopædia Britannica's President on Killing Off a 244-Year-Old Product," *Harvard Business Review*, 2013.

[133] Wikimedia Statistics, "Wikimedia Statistics," November 2020. [Online]. Available: https://stats.wikimedia.org/#/all-projects.

[134] Alexa, "The top 500 sites on the web," Alexa, 2021. [Online]. Available: https://www.alexa.com/topsites.

[135] S. Nadella, *Hit Refresh: The Quest to Rediscover Microsoft's Soul and Imagine a Better Future for Everyone*, Harper Business, 2017.

[136] Business Insider, "Satya Nadella employed a 'growth mindset' to overhaul Microsoft's cutthroat culture and turn it into a trillion-dollar company—here's how he did it," *Business Insider*, 3 July 2020. [Online]. Available: https://www.businessinsider.fr/us/microsoft-ceo-satya-nadella-company-culture-shift-growth-mindset-2020-3.

[137] J. Novet, "How Satya Nadella tripled Microsoft's stock price in just over four years," CNBC, 18 July 2018. [Online]. Available: https://www.cnbc.com/2018/07/17/how-microsoft-has-evolved-under-satya-nadella.html.

[138] J. Davis, "How LEGO clicked: the super brand that reinvented itself," *The Guardian*, 4 June 2017. [Online]. Available: https://www.theguardian.com/lifeandstyle/2017/jun/04/how-lego-clicked-the-super-brand-that-reinvented-itself.

[139] Wikipedia, "The LEGO Movie," January 2021. [Online]. Available: https://en.wikipedia.org/wiki/The_Lego_Movie.

[140] 2. Anthony Ha•August 4, "Disney+ grows to more than 60.5M subscribers," Techcrunch, 4 August 2020. [Online]. Available: https://techcrunch.com/2020/08/04/disney-grows-to-more-than-60-5m-subscribers/.

[141] C. Framke, "Disney announces it's ditching Netflix to start its own streaming service," VOX, 8 August 2017. [Online]. Available: https://www.vox.com/culture/2017/8/8/16115544/disney-netflix-distribution-deal-marvel.

[142] M. Dowd, "The Slow-Burning Success of Disney's Bob Iger," *The New York Times*, 26 September 2019. [Online]. Available: https://www.nytimes.com/2019/09/22/style/disney-bob-iger-book.html?module=inline.

[143] A. Carr, "What Hotel Operators Really Think Of Airbnb," *Fast Company*, 20 March 2014. [Online]. Available: https://www.fastcompany.com/3027976/what-hotel-operators-really-think-of-airbnb.

[144] R. G. McGrath, "The New Disrupters," *MIT Sloan Management Review*, no. Spring 2020.

[145] Statista, "Value of the global eyewear market from 2019 to 2027," Statista, 30 November 2020. [Online]. Available: https://www.statista.com/statistics/300087/global-eyewear-market-value/.

[146] Warby Parker, "History," Warby Parker, n.d.. [Online]. Available: https://www.warbyparker.com/history.

[147] "Warby Parker," 2021. [Online]. Available: https://www.warbyparker.com/.

[148] "Interview with Neil Blumenthal and Dave Gilboa," 5 December 2011. [Online]. Available: https://www.youtube.com/watch?v=b2ZZGbnweFI&feature=emb_imp_woyt.

[149] E. Siegel, "How Warby Parker disrupted the $140B eyewear industry," Disruption Mag, 17 May 2016. [Online]. Available: https://disruptionmag.com/2016/05/17/dave-gilboa-warby-parker/.

[150] Warby Parker, "Home Try on," Warby Parker, n.d.. [Online]. Available: https://www.warbyparker.com/home-try-on.

[151] A. Pardes, "Try on Your Next Pair of Glasses Using Just Your iPhone," *WIRED*, 2 February 2019. [Online]. Available: https://www.wired.com/story/warby-parker-augmented-reality-app/.

[152] Warby Parker, "Buy a pair give a pair," Warby Parker, n.d.. [Online]. Available: https://www.warbyparker.com/buy-a-pair-give-a-pair.

[153] Warby Parker, "Impact Report 2019," Warby Parker, 2019.

[154] J. Crook, "Warby Parker, valued at $3 billion, raises $245 million in funding," TechCrunch, 27 August 2020. [Online]. Available: https://techcrunch.com/2020/08/27/warby-parker-valued-at-3-billion-raises-245-million-in-funding/.

[155] J. Lim, "Canva Carries Out 7 Year Vision To Disrupt Digital Design," *Forbes*, 15 May 2015. [Online]. Available: https://www.forbes.com/sites/jlim/2015/05/07/canva-carries-out-7-year-vision-to-disrupt-digital-design/?sh=1d53a2e6744d.

[156] Canva, "Canva Pricing," Canva, 2021. [Online]. Available: https://www.canva.com/pricing/.

[157] Canva, "About Canva," 2021. [Online]. Available: https://about.canva.com/diversity/.

[158] L. Kim, "10 Facts About Canva CEO Melanie Perkins," Inc., 23 July 2019. [Online]. Available: https://www.inc.com/larry-kim/10-facts-about-canva-ceo-melanie-perkins.html.

[159] A. Konrad, "Canva Uncovered: How A Young Australian Kitesurfer Built A $3.2 Billion (Profitable!) Startup Phenom," *Forbes Magazine*, 31 December 2019. [Online]. Available: https://www.forbes.com/sites/alexkonrad/2019/12/11/inside-canva-profitable-3-billion-startup-phenom/?sh=3dd4786e4a51.

[160] Which 50, "In Two Years Canva's Value Has Surged From One To Six Billion," Which 50, 23 June 2020. [Online]. Available: https://which-50.com/in-two-years-canvas-value-has-surged-from-one-to-six-billion/.

[161] S. Thomsen, "Canva just doubled in value to $8.7bn on an $87 million raise," Startup Daily, 23 June 2020. [Online]. Available: https://www.startupdaily.net/2020/06/canva-just-doubled-in-value-to-8-7bn-on-an-87-million-raise/.

[162] Wikipedia, "Blockbuster LLC," 2020. [Online]. Available: https://en.wikipedia.org/wiki/Blockbuster_LLC.

[163] DOER one for all, "Netflix, the 'Amazon of Entertainment'," 2021. [Online]. Available: http://doerlife.com/netflix-the-amazon-of-entertainment/.

[164] D. Bennett, "Kodak Files for Bankruptcy," *The Atlantic*, 19 January 2012. [Online]. Available: https://www.theatlantic.com/business/archive/2012/01/kodak-files-bankruptcy/332934/.

[165]   Y. Noguchi, "Why Borders Failed While Barnes & Noble Survived," npr, 19 July 2011. [Online]. Available: https://www.npr.org/2011/07/19/138514209/why-borders-failed-while-barnes-and-noble-survived?t=1566156169991.

[166]   N. Brown, "Borders' IP sale to Barnes & Noble on hold," Reuters, 22 September 2011. [Online]. Available: https://www.reuters.com/article/us-borders/borders-ip-sale-to-barnes-noble-on-hold-idUSTRE78L6KL20110922.

[167]   Y. Doz, "The Strategic Decisions That Caused Nokia's Failure," Insead Knowledge, 23 November 2017. [Online]. Available: https://knowledge.insead.edu/strategy/the-strategic-decisions-that-caused-nokias-failure-7766.

[168]   S. Levinson, "Abercrombie Says It Would Rather Burn Clothes Than Give Them To Poor People," elite daily, 9 May 2013. [Online]. Available: https://www.elitedaily.com/news/world/abercrombie-says-it-would-rather-burn-clothes-than-give-them-to-poor-people.

[169]   Z. Kleinman, "Why our ageing social networks may need TikTok," BBC News, 4 December 2020. [Online].

[170]   Wikipedia, "Tik Tok," [Online]. Available: https://en.wikipedia.org/wiki/TikTok#:~:text=Douyin%20was%20launched%20by%20ByteDance,fifth%20of%20Internet%20users%20globally..

[171]   A. North, "50 Stats & Facts That Show How TikTok Will Define The Future Of Privacy & Social Media," Whats the host, 19 August 2020. [Online]. Available: https://www.whatsthehost.com/tiktok-stats/.

[172] P. Leskin, "TikTok surpasses 2 billion downloads and sets a record for app installs in a single quarter," *Business Insider*, 30 April 2020. [Online]. Available: https://www.businessinsider.fr/us/tiktok-app-2-billion-downloads-record-setting-q1-sensor-tower-2020-4#:~:text=TikTok%20has%20surpassed%202%20billion,had%20in%20a%20single%20quarter..

[173] M. Iqbal, "TikTok Revenue and Usage Statistics (2021)," Business of Apps, 10 February 2021. [Online]. Available: https://www.businessofapps.com/data/tik-tok-statistics/.

[174] Wikipedia, "Microsoft," [Online]. Available: https://en.wikipedia.org/wiki/Microsoft.

[175] R. Fannin, "The Strategy Behind TikTok's Global Rise," *Harvard Business Review*, 13 September 2019. [Online]. Available: https://hbr.org/2019/09/the-strategy-behind-tiktoks-global-rise.

[176] L. J. M. a. W. Lu, "Gen Z Is Set to Outnumber Millennials Within a Year," Bloomberg, 20 August 2018. [Online]. Available: https://www.bloomberg.com/news/articles/2018-08-20/gen-z-to-outnumber-millennials-within-a-year-demographic-trends.

[177] CB INSIGHTS, "How TikTok's Owner Became The World's Most Valuable Unicorn," CBINSIGHTS, 18 June 2020. [Online]. Available: https://www.cbinsights.com/research/report/bytedance-tiktok-unicorn/.

[178] Bloomberg News, "Bytedance Is Said to Secure Funding at Record $75 Billion Value," Bloomberg, 26 October 2018. [Online].

[179] "TikTok Money Calculator [Influencer Engagement & Earnings Estimator]," 12 March 2021. [Online]. Available: https://influencermarketinghub.com/tiktok-money-calculator/.

[180] C. Chan, "The rise of AI as a product" consumer apps," Reforge, 20 December 2018. [Online]. Available: https://www.reforge.com/brief/why-monthly-user-churn-is-a-terrible-metric#EONT1KFxuKmzYxnCQ21kkA.

[181] M. V. A. Y. Jason P. Davis, "TikTok's AI Strategy: ByteDance's Global Ambitions," Insead, 2019.

[182] Statista, "Number of TikTok downloads from 1st quarter 2017 to 1st quarter 2020," Statista, 4 February 2021. [Online]. Available: https://www.statista.com/statistics/1116267/tiktok-worldwide-downloads-quarterly/.

[183] "How TikTok's Owner Became The World's Most Valuable Unicorn," 2020. [Online]. Available: https://www.cbinsights.com/research/report/bytedance-tiktok-unicorn/.

[184] Angry Grammarian, "How coronavirus made 'zoom' a verb and other ways the pandemic has changed our language | The Angry Grammarian," *The Philadelphia Inquirer*, 29 April 2020. [Online]. Available: https://www.inquirer.com/opinion/coronavirus-covid-zoom-pandemic-words-linguistic-20200429.html.

[185] Reuters, "Zoom says it has 300 million daily meeting participants, not users," Reuters, 30 April 2020. [Online]. Available: https://www.reuters.com/article/us-zoom-video-commn-encryption/zoom-says-it-has-300-million-meeting-participants-not-users-idUSKBN22C1T4.

[186] K. Clark, "Zoom, a profitable unicorn, files to go public," Techcrunch, 22 March 2019. [Online]. Available: https://techcrunch.com/2019/03/22/zoom-a-profitable-unicorn-files-to-go-public/.

[187] Zoom, "How Our Customer Success Team Uses Zoom to Deliver Happiness," Zoom Blog, 25 July 2019. [Online]. Available: https://blog.zoom.us/customer-success-team-uses-zoom-to-deliver-happiness/.

[188] B. Fung, "Facebook and Google are coming for Zoom," CNN Business, 30 April 2020. [Online]. Available: https://edition.cnn.com/2020/04/30/tech/zoom-google-facebook/index.html.

[189] Startup Grind 2019, "Erick Yuan CEO of ZOOM on How To Break Monopoly," 19 April 2019. [Online]. Available: https://www.youtube.com/watch?v=f7E_YhOxnA4.

[190] Zoom, "Zoom Pricing," 2020. [Online]. Available: https://zoom.us/pricing.

[191] J. Chao, "Zoom Aims to Disrupt Video Conferencing Market," 18 July 2013. [Online]. Available: https://www.enterprisenetworkingplanet.com/unified_communications/zoom-aims-to-disrupt-video-conferencing-market.html.

[192] Statista, "Number of sent and received e-mails per day worldwide from 2017 to 2024," Statista, 2 October 2020. [Online]. Available: https://www.statista.com/statistics/456500/daily-number-of-e-mails-worldwide/.

[193] .E. Kim, "Here's another chart that shows Slack's incredible growth," *Business Insider*, 19 May 2015. [Online]. Available: https://www.businessinsider.com/heres-another-chart-that-shows-slacks-incredible-growth-2015-5?IR=T.

[194] "Stewart Butterfield," Wikipedia, [Online]. Available: https://en.wikipedia.org/wiki/Stewart_Butterfield.

[195] Slack, "Moving beyond remote: Workplace transformation in the wake of COVID-19," Slack, 20 October 2020. [Online]. Available: https://slack.com/intl/en-gb/blog/collaboration/workplace-transformation-in-the-wake-of-covid-19.

[196] D. Curry, "Slack Revenue and Usage Statistics (2020)," Business of Apps, 2 December 2020. [Online]. Available: https://www.businessofapps.com/data/slack-statistics/#:~:text=While%20Slack%20has%20grown%20steadily,currently%20at%2075%20million%20DAUs..

[197] C. Higgins, "Ridiculous U.K. Traffic Laws of Yore," MF, 22 November 2015. [Online]. Available: https://www.mentalfloss.com/article/71555/ridiculous-uk-traffic-laws-yore.

[198]　G. Hamel, "The Hole in the Soul of Business," *The Wall Street Journal*, 13 January 2010. [Online]. Available: https://www.wsj.com/articles/BL-GHMB-149.

[199]　J. P. K. &. J. L. Heskett, *Corporate Culture and Performance*, New York: Free Press, 1992.

[200]　R. Henderson, "Sustainability is an innovation problem," Digital Initiative—Harvard Business School, 12 September 2019. [Online]. Available: https://digital.hbs.edu/innovation-disruption/sustainability-is-an-innovation-problem/.

[201]　IBM Institute for Business Value, "Meet 2020 consumers driving change," 2020.

[202]　S. Mainwaring, "Purpose At Work: How Seventh Generation Accelerates Sustainable Growth," *Forbes*, 30 April 2019. [Online]. Available: https://www.forbes.com/sites/simonmainwaring/2019/04/30/purpose-at-work-how-seventh-generation-accelerates-sustainable-growth/?sh=7eb56f581547.

[203]　Accenture, "Accenture Strategy's most recent global survey," Accenture, 5 December 2018. [Online]. Available: https://www.accenture.com/cz-en/insights/strategy/brand-purpose.

[204]　V. Sonsev, "Patagonia's Focus On Its Brand Purpose Is Great For Business," *Forbes*, 17 November 2019. [Online]. Available: https://www.forbes.com/sites/veronikasonsev/2019/11/27/patagonias-focus-on-its-brand-purpose-is-great-for-business/?sh=3f5aed8754cb.

[205]　J. Fromm, "The Purpose Series: Ben & Jerry's Authentic Purpose," *Forbes*, 4 June 2019. [Online]. Available: https://www.forbes.com/sites/jefffromm/2019/06/04/the-purpose-series-ben-jerrys-authentic-purpose/?sh=514c2ec75bad.

[206]　CNBC, "CNBC DISRUPTOR 50," CNBC, 16 June 2020. [Online]. Available: https://www.cnbc.com/2020/06/16/tala-disruptor-50.html.

[207] M&S, "M&S Helps Customers to 'Think Climate' By Relabelling Clothing," April 2007. [Online]. Available: https://corporate.marksandspencer.com/media/press-releases/archive/2007/23042007_mshelpscustomerstothinkclimatebyrelabellingclothing.

[208] S. Nagarajan, "$82 trillion over 5 years? Cambridge study counts the cost of coronavirus," World Economic Forum, 27 May 2020. [Online]. Available: https://www.weforum.org/agenda/2020/05/coronavirus-covid19-pandemic-economamy-money-depression-recession/.

[209] United Nations Development Program, "What are the Sustainable Development Goals?" 2020. [Online]. Available: https://www.undp.org/content/undp/en/home/sustainable-development-goals.html#:~:text=The%20Sustainable%20Development%20Goals%20(SDGs,peace%20and%20prosperity%20by%202030..

[210] WE-ECONOMY, "Clothing that grows with your child," [Online]. Available: https://we-economy.net/case-stories/vigga.html

[211] The Bible, The Story of David and Goliath - Psalm 62:6.

[212] World Wide Words, "Elephant in the room," [Online]. Available: http://www.worldwidewords.org/qa/qa-ele2.htm.

[213] United Nations, "THE 17 GOALS," [Online]. Available: https://sdgs.un.org/goals.

[214] National Geographic, "Anthropocene," 2020. [Online]. Available: https://www.nationalgeographic.org/encyclopedia/anthropocene/.

[215] J. Bowen, "Beethoven as Bill Gates," TEDxSMU, December 2011. [Online]. Available: https://www.ted.com/talks/jose_bowen_beethoven_the_businessman.

[216] IBM, "IBM Watson is AI for business," n.d.. [Online]. Available: https://www.ibm.com/watson.

[217] Facebook, "Facebook at the 2020 Conference on Computer Vision and Pattern Recognition," 2020. [Online]. Available: https://research.fb.com/conferences/conference-on-computer-vision-and-pattern-recognition-cvpr-2020/.

[218] OpenMind BBVA, "Fully Autonomous Cars. How and When Will They Become a Reality?," 30 November 2020. [Online]. Available: https://www.bbvaopenmind.com/en/technology/innovation/fully-autonomous-cars-how-and-when-will-become-reality/.

[219] S. Marcacci, "Renewable Energy Prices Hit Record Lows: How Can Utilities Benefit From Unstoppable Solar And Wind?," Forbes, 21 January 2020. [Online]. Available: https://www.forbes.com/sites/energyinnovation/2020/01/21/renewable-energy-prices-hit-record-lows-how-can-utilities-benefit-from-unstoppable-solar-and-wind/?sh=7271a4542c84.

[220] Food and Agriculture Organization of the United Nations, "The future of food and agriculture: Trends and Challenges," 2017. [Online]. Available: http://www.fao.org/3/a-i6583e.pdf.

[221] M. Cole, "The future of food," CSIROscope, 17 August 2017. [Online]. Available: https://blog.csiro.au/the-future-of-food/.

[222] The Medical Futurist, "The Future of Food and Eating," 11 August 2020. [Online]. Available: https://medicalfuturist.com/the-future-of-food-the-food-of-the-future/.

[223] B. Morgan, "The Fashion Industry Is Ready For A Makeover: 4 Changes We'll See In The Future," *Forbes*, 3 December 2020. [Online]. Available: https://www.forbes.com/sites/blakemorgan/2020/12/03/the-fashion-industry-is-ready-for-a-makeover-4-changes-well-see-in-the-future/?sh=55120a60914a.

[224] Khan Academy, [Online]. Available: https://www.khanacademy.org/.